MARINE LIFE OF THE NORTH ATLANTIC

Canada to New England

—Third Edition—

Text and Photography:

ANDREW J. MARTINEZ

Edited by Candace Storm Martinez

Aqua Quest Publications, Inc. ■ New York

Other Aqua Quest Titles Available

Ask your dive center or book store for other titles by Aqua Quest Publications, publishers of books on dive travel destinations, underwater photography and videography, wreck diving, dive-related fiction, marine life and technical diving. Please visit our web site for a description of available titles, or contact us for a catalog of our publications.

Aqua Quest Publications, Inc.
Post Office Box 700
Locust Valley, NY 11560-0700

(800) 933-8989 (516) 759-0476
Fax: (516) 759-4519 E Mail: catalog@aquaquest.com

www.aquaquest.com

Contact the Author

The author welcomes your comments and suggestions. You may reach him at: www.andrewjmartinez.com

Library of Congress Cataloging-in-Publication Data

Martinez, Andrew J., 1946-
Marine Life of the North Atlantic : Canada to New England / Text and photography Andrew J. Martinez; edited by Candance Storm Martinez — 3rd ed.
p. cm.
Includes bibliographical references (p.) and index.
ISBN 1-881652-32-7 : $30.00 (pbk.)
1. Marine organisms—Atlantic Coast (New England)—Identification. 2. Marine organisms—Atlantic Coast (Canada)—Identification. I. Martinez, Candance Storm. II. Title.
QH104.5.N4 M28 2002
578.77'34—dc21

2002015844

Printed In China

10 9 8 7 6 5 4 3 2 1

To my mother Maria, for her love and kindness;
to the memory of my father Andres, from whom
I gained a love and fascination of the sea;
and to my uncle Tony, my tireless supporter.

AUTHOR'S NOTE

Marine Life of the North Atlantic is a product of my interest in photography and my love of the sea. While diving and photographing over the years, I needed just this kind of identification book for our region, but none was available. I often wanted a book which included information and photographs about reproduction, feeding, and unique behavior as well as color variations within a species. Hopefully, this user-friendly book will fill the needs of others whose interest is to seek and identify. Perhaps this book will create or maintain in the reader the excitement for North Atlantic waters that I still feel each time I dive. After twenty-five years, this is still my favorite underwater area.

So, get yourself to the beach. Look carefully among the rocks and crevices. Watch the amazing show that Nature provides. I can only hope that you find excitement and pleasure each time you visit and that *Marine Life of the North Atlantic* will add to your enjoyment.

—Andrew J. Martinez

ACKNOWLEDGMENTS

Many people were instrumental in the preparation of this book. Particular thanks go to Richard Harlow of Tabor Academy for his help with the botany section and for his work in the original *Marine Life of the North Atlantic.* The editing of David Donavel, Cynthia Harlow, and scientific editing of Dr. Charles Kellogg are greatly appreciated. Special thanks to Anthony Constantino for final editing of the entire book. Special appreciation to graphic designer Susan Haas for outstanding illustrations. Thanks to Tricia Deforge for her technical skill in putting it all together.

I am grateful to the following friends who gave their time and assistance: Zachary Zevitas for much needed suggestions in the early stages; Richard Taylor and Gina Tremblay for finding some of the creatures; Wan Chi Lau for technical assistance; and Harvey Petersiel and Fred Bavendam for guidance and support through the years. Further thanks to Fred Dion of Underwater Photo-Tech for keeping the cameras in good working order and always being willing to help. For all my friends in the diving industry, your support of the original book is deeply appreciated.

Special thanks to the scientific community for generously giving their time and expert help with specific animals: Dr. Nathan Riser, Northeastern University Nahant Marine Laboratory, for nudibranchs and tunicates; Dr. Laurence P. Madin, Woods Hole Oceanographic Institution, for hydromedusae; Dr. Patricia Morse, Northeastern University Nahant Marine Laboratory, and Dr. Alan Kuzirian, Woods Hole Oceanographic Institution, for nudibranchs; and Dr. Richard Harbison, Woods Hole Oceanographic Institution, for ctenophores.

Requests for information were generously and patiently responded to by the following people: Dr. Larry G. Harris, University of New Hampshire, who was extremely patient and helpful with my many inquiries; Dr. John Costello, Providence College, who also answered hours of questions; Edward Enos, Marine Biological Laboratory, Woods Hole, for guidance and encouragement; and Ted Maney, Northeastern University Nahant Marine Laboratory, was very helpful identifying some of the marine animals.

The following people welcomed me to their collections, libraries, or aquariums to do research: Karsten Hartel, Curator of Fishes, Harvard University; Donald Flescher, NOAA, Woods Hole; and Paul Connon, Aquarium at Woods Hole. A very special thanks to Dr. Ruth Turner, Harvard University, a wonderful person who offered support, suggestions, and helpful criticism. Thanks also to Jerry Prezioso, NOAA, Narragansett, Rhode Island, for finding great Rhode Island marine life on some wonderful dives.

The biggest thanks go to my wife, Candace. Without her help this book would not be what it is today. Yes, I had the photos and wrote the text but it was her careful eye, critical editing, rewriting, and unfailing support that helped me put it together.

Special mention of two dive buddies who have sadly passed away: Norman Katz, whose enthusiasm and effort helped with the first book, and Norman Despres, a diver, contributing photographer, and friend who is greatly missed. I would like to thank the following underwater photographers, who donated the use of their images for this book. Most are long-time diving friends who have contributed in many other ways to the project:

Photo Credits:

Fred Bavendam: pgs. 53, 75, 119, 227, 229, 231; **Robert Boyle:** pgs. 49, 109, 217, 251, 253; **Norman Despres:** pgs. 45, 183, 187; **Adam Geiger:** pgs. 67, 147, 183, 221; **Laurence Madin:** pg. 47; **Roger Mooers:** pg. 99; **David Norman:** pg. 59; **Richard Palanzi:** pg. 135; **Jerry Prezioso:** pgs. 173, 221, 227; **Herb Segars:** pgs. 47, 73, 233, 243; **Richard Sperry:** pg. 221; **David Whittemore:** pgs. 139, 247; **Paul Young:** pg. 147. All other photographs were taken by the author, **Andrew J. Martinez**.

Credits:

Editor: Candace S. Martinez

Layout and Design: Tricia Deforge

Illustrations: Susan Haas

Cover Design and Map: Chris Zarza

SUGGESTIONS FOR USING THIS BOOK:

This easy-to-use guide is designed to help you identify many species found in North Atlantic waters. It covers marine plants and animals from the arctic reaches of eastern Canada to the waters of southern New England. In most cases, common representative species are featured. It would be difficult, as well as financially impossible, to include photographs of all the creatures found in these waters.

Identifying a marine plant or animal that is found on the beach or underwater can be very confusing to a beginning observer. After you use an identification guide for a while, you will notice that there are major groupings, called *phyla* (singular, *phylum*), of plants and animals. Each phylum includes organisms with similar physical characteristics. Often, an organism fits into its group in ways that can be observed; but sometimes the reasons are more scientific and cannot be observed. In either case, this book's description of each phylum will give you some general information about the group of plants or animals whose pictures are to follow. The opening text of each section may be a good place to start.

In your marine investigations, you may recognize an organism that fits into a particular phylum, but you may not know its name. Go directly to the phylum and search the pictures for a similar plant or animal. If you do know the animal's name, look in the index to find it. Two indices—Common Names and Scientific Names—are included. Most organisms are arranged in the proper taxonomical order within the book (from the least complex to the most complex). Due to limits imposed by the design of this book, a few creatures are somewhat out of order but are listed within their correct phylum.

For each plant and animal entry, physical features are described in **Identification. Habitat** indicates the underwater environment in which the organism can be found. **Range** describes its distribution along the coast from Canada to New England. **Comments** may include similar species, special behavior, or confusing field characteristics. Again:

- To find out about the characteristics of each phylum, or group, read the text at the beginning of each section.
- If you know the phylum that the organism is in, check the Table of Contents for the section. Then, look through the photos until you find it.
- If you know the name of the organism, check one of the two indices (Common Names or Scientific Names).
- If you are unfamiliar with a term used in the descriptions, check the Glossary, which begins on page 256.
- To find out where an animal fits in the "big picture," check the Outline of Taxonomy.
- Keep a record of when and where you first saw the organism. Use the space to the right of the photos to record your data.
- Take this book with you when you go walking, snorkeling, or diving. By getting to know the organisms you see, you will appreciate them more.

OUTLINE OF TAXONOMY

Plant Kingdom:

DIVISION: CYANOPHYTA—**blue-green algae**
DIVISION: CHLOROPHYTA—**green algae**
DIVISION: PHAEOPHYTA—**brown algae**
DIVISION: RHODOPHYTA—**red algae**
DIVISION: TRACHEOPHTYTA—**vascular plants**
    SUBDIVISION: Angiospermata—**seed plants**

Animal Kingdom:

PHYLUM: PORIFERA—**sponges**

PHYLUM: CNIDARIA—**polyps and medusae**
- CLASS: Hydrozoa—**hydroids**
  - ORDER: Siphonophora—**colonial jellyfish**
- CLASS: Scyphozoa—(true jellyfish) **moon jelly, lion's mane**
- CLASS: Anthozoa—**corals and sea anemones**
  - SUBCLASS: Hexacorallia
    - ORDER: Actiniaria—**anemones**
    - ORDER: Cerianthida—**tube anemones**
  - SUBCLASS: Octocorallina—**soft corals**

PHYLUM: CTENOPHORA—**comb jellies**

PHYLUM: RHYNCHOCOELA—**nemertean worms**

PHYLUM: BRYOZOA—**bryozoans**

PHYLUM: BRACHIOPODA—**lamp shells**

PHYLUM: MOLLUSCA
- CLASS: Polyplacophora—**chitons**
- CLASS: Gastropoda—(one shell) **snails, limpets, nudibranchs**
- CLASS: Bivalvia—**clams, mussels, oysters**
- CLASS: Cephalopoda—**squid, octopuses**

PHYLUM: ANNELIDA—**segmented worms**
- CLASS: Polychaeta—**bristle worms**
  - SUBCLASS: Sedentaria—**hard worms, teribellid worms**
  - SUBCLASS: Errantia—**clam worm, paddle worms**

PHYLUM: ARTHROPODA—**jointed-leg**
- CLASS: Pantopoda—**sea spiders**
- CLASS: Merostomata—**horseshoe crabs**
- CLASS: Crustacea—**shrimps, lobsters, crabs, barnacles, isopods**
- CLASS: Chilopoda—**centipedes**
- CLASS: Diplopoda—**millipedes**
- CLASS: Insecta—**insects**

PHYLUM: ECHINODERMATA—**spiny skinned**
- CLASS: Stelleroidea—**stars**
  - SUBCLASS: Asteroidea—**sea stars**
  - SUBCLASS: Ophiuroidea—**brittle stars, basket stars**
- CLASS: Echinoidea—**sea urchins, sand dollars**
- CLASS: Holothuroidea—**scarlet psolus and other sea cucumbers**
- CLASS: Crinoidea—**crinoids**

PHYLUM: CHORDATA
- SUBPHYLUM: Urochordata—**tunicates**
- SUBPHYLUM: Vertebrata—**vertebrates**
  - CLASS: Chondrichthyes—**rays, skates, sharks**
  - CLASS: Osteichthyes—**all bony fish**

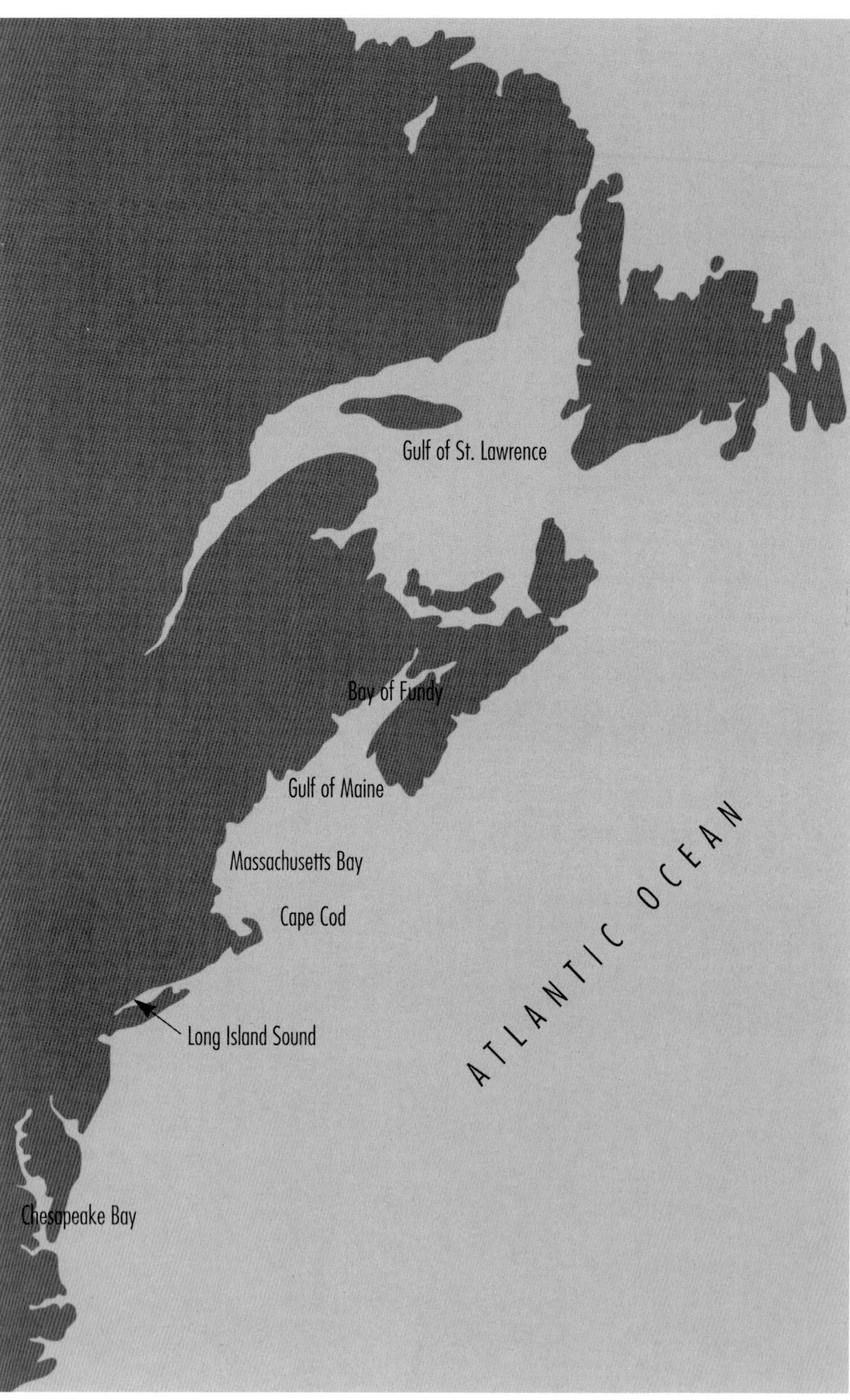
Gulf of St. Lawrence
Bay of Fundy
Gulf of Maine
Massachusetts Bay
Cape Cod
Long Island Sound
ATLANTIC OCEAN
Chesapeake Bay

LIFE ZONES

Marine Life of the North Atlantic is a guidebook for the seashore visitor and diver from Atlantic Canada to New England. It covers life that can be found in tide pools, on beaches, in shallow water, or within easy visual reach by snorkeling or diving. In biogeographical terms, the region from Labrador to Cape Cod is called the "American Atlantic Boreal Region." It is greatly influenced by the Labrador Current, a cold water "stream" or "river" that keeps our northern coastal waters cold. The "American Atlantic Temperate Region" extends south from Cape Cod to Cape Hatteras, a life zone influenced by the warmer waters of the Gulf Stream. The primary focus of this book is marine life that falls within the American Atlantic Boreal Region, although some of the listed organisms may be found farther south than New England.

The range of an organism is considered to be the area where environmental factors favor its growth. It is usually bounded by northern and southern limits. The land mass of Cape Cod is considered by some references as the southern limit of most Boreal species and as the northern limit of most Temperate species, but this is not true for every species. Another factor for consideration is the depth of water. Some animals live on or around marine plants that are only found in the shallower waters near the coastline. Other animals can only live within a narrow range of temperature. Species that can be found close to shore in cold, northern waters may also be found farther south, but at greater depths where the water is similarly cold.

The habitat of an organism includes all the environmental factors that allow it to live in a particular location. In short, it is the place where an organism lives. The habitat includes other living organisms as well as the nonliving environment. Environmental factors in a marine environment can include temperature, salinity, depth, substrate, and type of coastline.

In this book, range and habitat are described for each entry. A particular organism may be found widely distributed within a range; it may be found in a variety of habitats, or in a particular habitat within that geographical area. Other organisms may have a more limited range, often with a habitat that is specifically suited to its survival. Climates, currents, and environments change, and the range of an organism may change correspondingly. As conditions become favorable to an organism in areas where it was previously not found, it may be able to colonize and live successfully, thereby extending its range.

TABLE OF CONTENTS

Coastlines....11

Marine Plants....13

Porifera (Sponges)....30

Cnidaria (Hyroids, Anemones, Corals)....38

Ctenophora (Comb Jellies)....70

Nemertea (Worms)....70

Bryozoa (Bryozoans)....71

Brachiopods (Lamp Shells)....71

Molluska (Gastropods, Nudibranch, Bivalves)....78

Annelida (Polychaetes, Segmented Worms)....132

Arthropoda (Crabs, Shrimps, Lobsters)....144

Echinodermata (Stars, Urchins, Cucumbers)....176

Chorata (Tunicates)....208

Chordata (Fish)....218

Glossary....256

Index – Common Names....264

Index – Scientific Names....269

Bibliography....271

COASTLINES

As any beach person knows, there is great variation in the shorelines of the coasts of any landmass. Shorelines have been created by different forces and continue to be influenced by elements that alter their form over the short and long term. Coastlines are formed of rock, sand, or mud, each having a diverse range of animals and plants that are perfectly suited for life in that particular physical environment. Of the three types of coastlines north of Cape Cod, the rocky shore is most common. Most of the creatures described and pictured in this book are found there. For that reason, the following discussion will detail more the character of the rocky shore while briefly mentioning sandy beaches and salt marshes. In no way does this imply that one coastal ecosystem is more important than the others, but interested readers should refer to other texts for more detail on these.

All shorelines have distinct zones that are defined by where the sea meets the land. This area between high tide and low tide is called the littoral, or intertidal, zone; the area above it, which receives wave splash and is never fully immersed, is the supralittoral zone; the area below it, which begins at the low spring tide line and goes out to sea, is the sublittoral zone. The distribution of plants and animals upon each individual shoreline and within each zone is subject to many influences—physical conditions (exposure, desiccation, temperature, salinity), competition for space between species and individuals, and predation by other species. All of these factors determine which organism has the right combination of adaptations to survive in a particular zone on a particular shoreline.

ROCKY SHORE—The rocky shore is in many ways a most appealing type, with its cliffs, inlets, tide pools, and crashing waves. It is the most stable or unchanging of the shorelines although wind, waves, and currents can alter the most resolute of rock over time. While looking around the panorama of the rocky shore, one can see colored, horizontal layers of biological zonation. These life zones are defined and named by the flora and/or fauna that thrive there.

Black Zone—This uppermost or supralittoral zone is defined by bacteria of the Calothrix species, which forms a dark band on coastal rocks. Calothrix is well suited to living in an area that is prone to extreme environmental conditions. It is able to secrete a sheathe of mucus that protects it and prevents it from drying out. The ability of Calothrix to stay moist makes the black zone a dangerous area to walk in, and one should take extreme care. Aside from Calothrix and a few filamentous green algae, relatively few species inhabit the supralittoral zone because of the challenges created by variations in temperature, salinity, and exposure. This is also where one will find the Rough Periwinkle, *Littorina saxitilis,* feeding on Calothrix or resting within a rock crevice.

White Zone—Beneath the black zone, the white zone is home to several species of barnacles. In this upper intertidal zone, organisms spend less time covered by salt water and are exposed to air much of the time. Species that are more tolerant to fluctuations in temperature and desiccation establish themselves higher in the intertidal zone, while similarly less tolerant species establish themselves in lower intertidal areas. *Balanus balanoides* is the most dominant species in this zone of the northwestern Atlantic. Other species of barnacles can be found in tide pools, on rocks, growing on a gastropod's shell, or on an arthropod's carapace.

Brown Zone—In the midtidal range, where organisms are submerged and exposed for about equal periods of time, a brown zone of life can be seen. It is primarily composed of two dominant alga species. Knotted Wrack, *Ascophyllum nodosum,* lives on rocks that are more sheltered and do not directly face ocean waves. It has a somewhat round thallus with single air bladders located some distance from each other along the stipe. Rockweed, *Fucus* *vesiculosis,* may occupy a place with moderate exposure to waves, as it is a shorter and tougher brown alga. *Fucus* has a flat thallus with a mid-rib, and paired air bladders lie on either side of the rib. Many species of brown algae have air bladders to help keep the thallus floating near the surface, where it can get the light needed for photosynthesis. These characteristic plants are visible at low tide as they hang down in a tangled mass from their holdfasts. In this forest of brown are many other lower intertidal species. Common Periwinkle, *Littorina littorea,* grazes on marine algae and takes refuge in the dark and damp environs that the brown seaweeds provide at low tide. Mats of Blue Mussels colonize rocks in places perhaps too rough for the Rockweed. Wherever there are barnacles and mussels, one can expect to see their predator, *Nucella lapillus,* the Dogwinkle.

Red Zone—Below the rockweed zone is the red zone, lowest in the intertidal area. Since this zone is out of water only a few hours each day, one can expect to see alga species that are less tolerant to desiccation and temperature extremes. It is characterized by red algae such as Irish Moss, *Chondrus crispus,* and Dulse, *Rhodymenia palmata.* Another marine alga found here is the green Sea Lettuce, *Ulva lactuca.* This zone also hosts the various crabs, urchins, stars, and anemones that define the lower intertidal zone. The end of this area marks the beginning of the subtidal zone, where one can find kelp species such as Laminaria and Alaria.

Tide pools, another feature of the rocky shore, can offer a personal observation laboratory to any patient investigator. They, too, host a variety of characteristic flora and fauna, depending upon their location. Tide pools high in the intertidal zone are flushed less regularly and usually support less life due to the extremes of temperature *and* salinity. Lower pools, which are flushed regularly by the tides, hold a variety of algae as well as more interesting creatures—from crabs and amphipods to hydroids and anemones.

SANDY BEACHES—More common from Cape Cod southward, these beaches consist of sand that has been broken down over time from the original granite and other rocks of the coast. Unlike the rocky shore, the sandy beach is different from day to day, from season to season, and before and after storms. The profile of a beach may be steep or gently sloping; it may have sand or pebbles or cobbles; it may have rough or gentle waves; it may have a barrier dune above the high tide line; and it will always have an intertidal zone between the high and low tide lines. Walking along the uppermost high tide line, one can see what the sea has brought in. One may find empty egg cases of whelks or skates, seaweeds knotted and tangled, empty shells of a snail or crab, pieces of a broken lobster trap, or tossed and smoothed beach glass. A knowledge of sand, waves, water currents, dunes, and barrier beaches is intrinsic to understanding a sand beach and its inhabitants. All of these deserve more time and space than can be devoted here.

SALT MARSHES—When a river flows into the sea, it creates a complex ecosystem dependent upon the ebb and flow of fresh, brackish (mixed fresh and salt), and salt water. This area is known as an estuary. The sheltered waters of bays and estuaries create conditions that favor the development of salt marshes. Salt marshes are considered to be muddy, mosquito producing, and foul smelling; indeed, they are all of these, but they are also considered to be some of the most productive land on Earth. In grossly simplified terms, the salt marsh is the compost bin and recycling area of the coastal sea. Within the shallow waters of every estuary, organic material from the ocean drops out of suspension and collects around the salt marsh plants, which are tolerant to the changes in salinity. These organic particles compact into a rich organic mud. Here, bacteria are at work breaking down the particles into compounds that nourish marine plants and animals. It is a complex recycling of the nutrients found in the sea. Many invertebrates (including shellfish) and fish spend a juvenile life stage here and give salt marshes their reputation as nurseries. The importance of the sheltered, gentle waters of the salt marsh cannot be underestimated; they are critical to the health of our entire marine ecosystem.

MARINE PLANTS

Algae are the single-celled and multi-celled plants of the sea. Commonly called seaweeds, they are usually more simple in structure than the seed-bearing plants of terrestrial (land) habitats. What they lack in complexity, however, they make up for in diversity, beauty, color, and tenacity.

Marine algae and sea grasses form the base of the marine food chain by converting sunlight and waterborne nutrients into plant material through photosynthesis. Whether they are single-celled planktonic or multi-celled macro algae, they provide oxygen, food, and habitat for most of the creatures of the sea, as well as creating oxygen that supports life on land.

Representatives from the three most often observed divisions (phyla) will be described and shown in this book. These are organized by the color of the algae: Chlorophyta (green), Phaeophyta (brown), and Rhodophyta (red). They all conduct photosynthesis and have chlorophylls (photosynthetic pigments). They may also contain other pigments, combinations of which make the colors of the algae remarkably diverse.

Color is a place to begin the identification process, but it may not be conclusive. The color of an alga is affected by its habitat and health. A plant that washes up on the beach may be brown, black, or white, giving little indication of its original color. For identification purposes, it is best to collect or observe living plants.

A typical seed-bearing plant (angiosperm) has a well-developed root structure, vascular (conductive) tissue, flowers, and seeds. Instead of a root structure, marine algae have developed holdfasts, which do just what the name implies. Holdfasts can be branched or disk-shaped. They attach firmly to the substrate, whether it is rock, wood, sand, or another alga. The stipe is a stem-like part that is present in many algae. It connects the holdfast to the blade, or frond, which is present in the kinds of algae that look "leafy." The blade is where most of the photosynthetic activity of the plant occurs. Many algae do not have a recognizable stipe, and the blade, or thallus (whole plant), may connect directly to the holdfast. Algae do not need vascular tissue in the same way that land plants do. They are surrounded by water that holds the nutrients and moisture that they need, so they do not need to take it in through roots. Algae may be annual, perennial, or year-round plants.

Two species of marine seed-bearing plants can be found in shallow and estuarine waters in the North Atlantic marine ecosystem. They are Eel Grass, *Zostera marina,* and Widgeon Grass, *Ruppia maritima.* Small flowers and seeds are present at some stage of the perennial cycle of both species. *Zostera* requires several years to mature. It is an important salt marsh plant that covers acres of shallow bays and provides food for ducks and habitat for small marine creatures.

Algae

Zonation on a rocky coast at low tide

GREEN FLEECE *Codium fragile*

Identification: This seaweed grows in large, rope-like, branching strands that are spongy and feel like wet felt. Dioecious. Color: green or yellow green with light green tips. Size: up to 3' (.9m).

Habitat: Grows on solid substrate, from sub-littoral to 40' (12m).

Range: Cape Ann, Massachusetts, to New Jersey. An isolated population exists in Boothbay Harbor, Maine.

Comments: When bleached by the sun as part of the flotsam on the beach, *Codium* looks like a white or gray-white piece of rope. Green Fleece is also known as "oyster thief" because it can interfere with the normal development of scallops and oysters. When *Codium* develops on an oyster or scallop shell and actively photosynthesizes, oxygen bubbles may be trapped in the plant; consequently, both *Codium* and the shellfish become buoyant and rise above the substrate. This action will eventually kill the mollusk. *Codium* was first seen in 1957 on eastern Long Island. Since then, it has gradually spread along our coast. At this point it is found growing abundantly throughout its range. Because it is so prolific, it has become a nuisance to boat owners and beachcombers alike.

HOLLOW GREEN ALGAE *Enteromorpha intestinalis*

Identification: Masses of hollow green tubes, usually seen with oxygen bubbles inside. Sometimes the coarse, hollow tubes are flattened, but in either case there are no branches. A hand lens cannot show the individual cells of this species. *E. intestinalsis* is the most common unbranched species and is the largest of its genus. Size: width, less than 1/16" (1.5mm) to more than 1" (25mm); length, more than 1' (30cm).

Habitat: Tide pools, intertidal to estuarine, with varied salinity tolerances. It will attach to a wide diversity of substrates and can be epiphytic.

Range: Arctic to Carolinas.

Comments: Other species of *Enteromorpha,* although having some characteristics in common, can be branched and are more restrictive in size. *E. compressa,* 5/8" (15mm) to 1" (25mm) wide, has basal branches and tolerates low salinity; *E. prolifera,* which is the same width as *E. compressa,* has scattered branches.

DATE

LOCATION

DATE

LOCATION

DATE

LOCATION

Algae

SEA LETTUCE *Ulva lactuca*

Identification: This alga looks like a large, flat, or rippled sheet of green that resembles a piece of lettuce. According to Kingsbury and Zottoli, *Ulva* grows profusely in areas that have a high nitrate concentration in the water. Color: bright green, sometimes yellow green, or blue green. Size: to 3' (.9m).

Habitat: Found in tide pools, intertidally to subtidally.

Range: Arctic to Long Island.

Comments: One can tell the difference between *Ulva* and *Monostroma,* which is similar in appearance, by doing the following: if you can see your fingerprint clearly through the algae, then you are looking at *Monostroma,* whose blades are only one cell thick. If you have difficulty seeing your fingerprint, then you are looking at *Ulva,* whose blades are two cells thick. *Ulva* should also feel heavy and sturdy, rather than thin and flimsy like *Monostroma.*

GREEN HAIR WEED *Chaetomorpha linum*

Identification: A filamentous, stiff, unbranched tangle of bright green threads whose cells are visible with a hand lens. It remains somewhat stiff out of water, feeling coarse to the touch, and is articulated with dark green bands. Color: bright green to yellow green. Size: 4" (102 mm).

Habitat: Found on sand or mud bottoms, intertidally to subtidally.

Range: Nova Scotia to Bermuda.

Similar Species: *Chaetomorpha melagonium* differs from *C. linum* in these ways: 1. its cells can be seen with the naked eye; 2. it has single, unbranched, coarse strands, usually 6" to 12" (15cm to 30cm); 3. it is partial to cold water; 4. it is found on rocks from the Arctic to New Jersey.

Green algae on a Moon Snail

DATE

LOCATION

DATE

LOCATION

DATE

LOCATION

Young *Fucus* sp.

SPIRAL ROCKWEED *Fucus spiralis*

Identification: This species is found *only* on the high side of the intertidal zone. It has winged receptacles (i.e., there is a thick rim of longitudinal cells around the receptacle) and no bladders. It shares the three characteristics that all fucoid species have in common: a disk-shaped holdfast, a prominent midrib, and a flattened thallus. Color: olive green to yellow brown. Size: to 3' (.9m).

Habitat: Rocky shores, upper littoral.

Range: Arctic to North Carolina.

Comments: Be careful about identifying this species simply by the ridge of tissue around the receptacles. New receptacles of *Fucus vesiculosus* may have this ridge, and old receptacles of *F. spiralis* may lack this ridge.

ROCKWEED *Fucus vesiculosus*

Identification: All Fucus species have three characteristics in common: a disk-shaped holdfast, a prominent midrib, and a flattened thallus. The most common of the rockweeds, *Fucus vesiculosus,* is the only one that has paired, pea-shaped air bladders (vesiculations) located at intervals on either side of a ribbed thallus. The mid-rib on a flattened thallus is characteristic of this species along with the dichotomously-branched blades. Color: olive green to yellow brown. Size: to 3' (.9m).

Habitat: Found on rocky shores, mid to lower littoral.

Range: Arctic to North Carolina.

Comments: Also known as Bladder Wrack, rockweed plants are either male or female. The oval-shaped receptacles found at the tips of the alga are olive green in the female and orange in the male. First appearing in the spring, they can stay on the plant for up to six months. Grows lower in the intertidal zone than *Ascophyllum.* Canopy species.

Similar species: *Fucus spiralis* has winged receptacles and no bladders, and it forms a narrow band at the upper levels of the intertidal zone. *Fucus distichus* (edentatus) is devoid of bladders, and its receptacles are long and flattened. This species tends to occupy the bottom of the brown zone, near the low tide mark.

DATE

LOCATION

DATE

LOCATION

DATE

LOCATION

Algae

KNOTTED WRACK *Ascophyllum nodosum*

Identification: This common algae is easily identified by its narrow, olive green to green black, adult, ribless blades, which bear thick-walled air bladders or "knots." Conspicuous along the irregular branches are small, short branchlets that project from the thallus except at the ends. Fruiting receptacles form on the ends of the larger branches in the fall and release sperm and eggs in early spring. The algae then shed these receptacles by the end of May. Size: to 3' (.9m).

Habitat: Quiet, rocky, intertidal water where there is minimal wave activity. Currents are not a problem for *Ascophyllum,* but intense wave action prevents this species from becoming established.

Range: Arctic to Long Island.

Comments: Canopy species that tends to be predominant in quiet, intertidal areas. Knotted Wrack is also known as Yellow Tang because it can be seen easily in murky water. This seaweed has both male and female plants. On the female plant, the gamete receptacles are yellowish. *Ascophyllum* is the specific epiphytic host to the red alga *Polysiphonia lanosa.*

***Ascophyllum nodosum*—**
reproductive (fruiting) receptacles

TUBED WEEDS *Polysiphonia lanosa*

Identification: This bushy, dark red alga consists of dense, stiff branches. Because the majority of the branches are the same length, the whole plant is somewhat round. When removed from the water, it maintains its shape and does not collapse. Color: dark red, almost black. Size: to 3" (76mm) in diameter. Epiphytic, primary host is *Ascophyllum nodosum.*

Habitat: Intertidal zone (see above).

Range: Arctic to Long Island.

DATE

LOCATION

DATE

LOCATION

DATE

LOCATION

Algae

SEA COLANDER *Agarum cribrosum*

Identification: This looks like a kelp that has been shot full of holes. Along with the branched holdfast, a relatively short stipe and an indistinct midrib characterize this unique alga. Color: rich, dark brown. Size: length, 3' to 4' (1m to 1.2m); width, 20" (50cm).

Habitat: Low tide to subtidal in the North, subtidal in the southern part of its range.

Range: Arctic to Cape Cod.

Comments: Also called Devil's Apron.

SOUTHERN KELP *Laminaria agardhii*

Identification: Long, flat blade whose edges are ruffled in the summer and flat in the winter. Its stipe is solid, relatively short, and it has a branching holdfast. On the inside of the light brown blade, there are two parallel lines of wart-like protrusions. This type of growth is also characteristic of other kelp species during the summer months. Color: light brown. Size: length, 10' (9m); width, 10" (25cm).

Habitat: Low tide to subtidal.

Range: Cape Cod south.

Comments: This kelp can establish a zone of its own at the low tide line. Similar species: *L. saccharina* can only be distinguished with the use of a microscope. *Saccorhiza dermatodea* has a cuplike holdfast rather than a branched holdfast. *Punctinaria* sp. have padlike holdfasts. Northern Kelp, *L. longicruris,* has a distinct and distally-inflated stipe from the holdfast, pinched before the blade.

A branched holdfast of *Laminaria.*

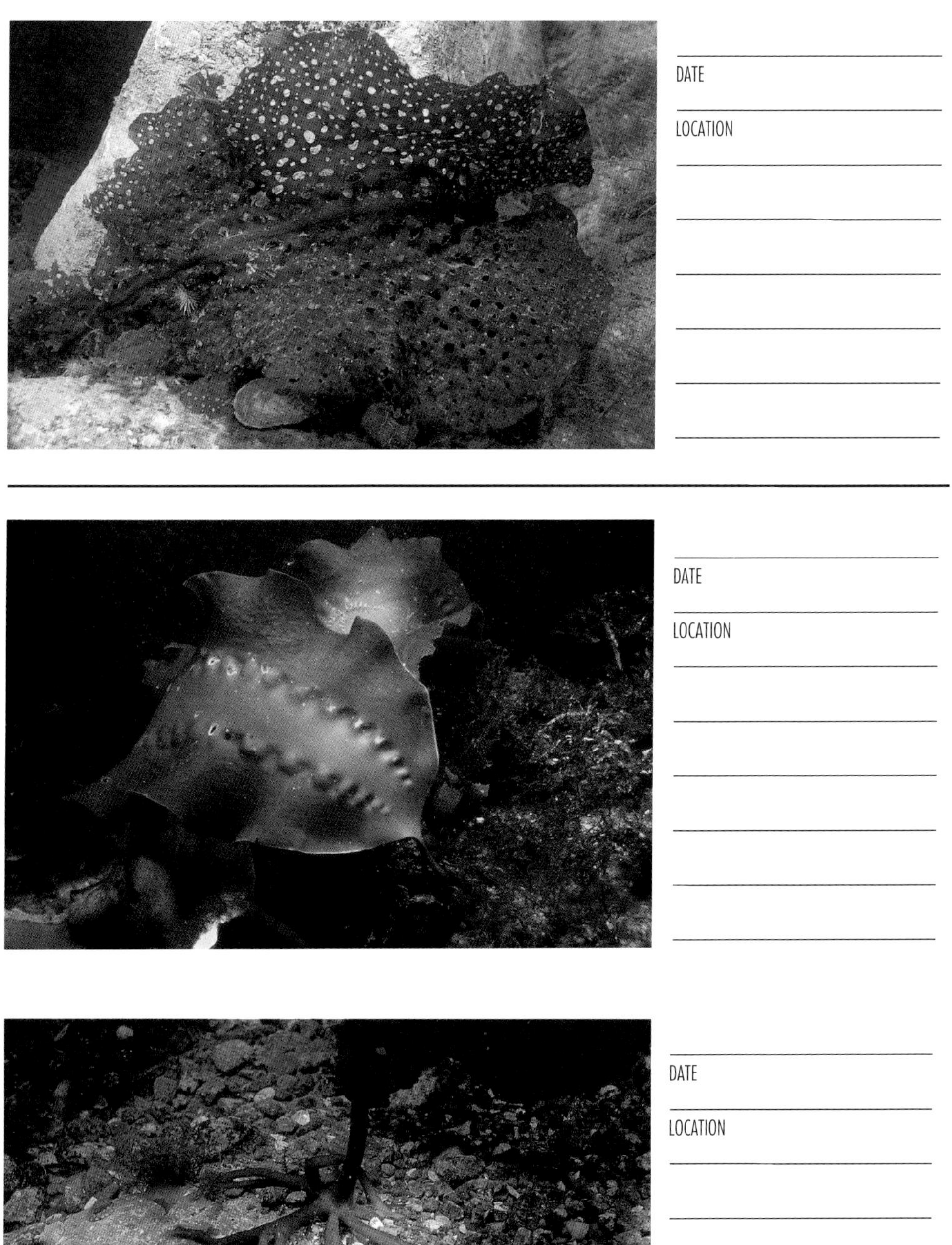

DATE

LOCATION

DATE

LOCATION

DATE

LOCATION

Algae

ROUGH TANGLE WEED *Stilophora rhizodes*

Identification: This is a rough, firm, somewhat brittle alga that is covered with warts on the branches. Color: soft yellow brown. Size: to 12" (30 cm).

Habitat: Found in quiet water, subtidally to shallow water.

Range: Nova Scotia to North Carolina.

Comments: Can be epiphytic.

SPINY SOUR WEED *Desmarestia aculeata*

Identification: There are two forms, a spring form and a summer form, and they look different from each other. The plant is plume-like with fine filaments during the spring, but in summer the filaments wear away while the alternating, spiny branchlets remain. Color: soft brown in spring, dark brown stem with lighter brown branchlets in summer. Size: to 18" (45 cm).

Habitat: Intertidally to subtidally.

Range: Arctic to Long Island Sound.

Comments: This is an annual weed that likes shallow, quiet water. Also known as Landlady's Wig.

CORAL WEED *Corallina officinalis*

Identification: This alga is noticeable because of its calcified segments. These are joined together by uncalcified joints, allowing it to sway back and forth with the currents and wave action. Color: pastel pink to purple red, with white tips on each branch. Size: to 4" (102mm).

Habitat: Found intertidally (in tide pools) to subtidally.

Range: Newfoundland to North Carolina.

Comments: When parts of this alga wash up on the beach, they bleach, eventually turning stark white and looking like beads.

DATE

LOCATION

DATE

LOCATION

DATE

LOCATION

Algae

IRISH MOSS *Chondrus crispus*

Identification: A dichotomously-branched alga. Each blade is flat and tapers to a single disc-shaped holdfast. *Chondrus* grows en masse on rocks, like turf. Color: deep red to reddish purple, varying to yellowish or yellow green when plants are near the surface and are exposed to intense sunlight. Size: length, 6" (155mm); width, 4" 102mm).

Habitat: Found intertidally to subtidally.

Range: Arctic to New Jersey.

Comments: This alga is harvested commercially for an extract called carrageenin, which is used as an emulsifier in many products including ice cream, toothpaste, baked goods, and cosmetics.

Irish Moss in intense light

Irish Moss in its more commonly found red coloration

HOOKED WEED *Bonnemaisonia hamifera*

Identification: A filamentous red alga that is usually found as part of the flotsom. It tends to grow in tangles and is often washed ashore. Key characteristics for identification are its color and the sickle-shaped hook at the end of some, but not all, of its many small branches. The hook is tapered to a sharp point. Color: rosy red. Size: to 4" (102mm).

Habitat: Below low tide to considerable depth.

Range: Cape Ann, Massachusetts to Long Island, New York.

Comments: Of our marine algae, only *Hypnea* is similarly structured, with hooks at the tip of branches. However, *Hypnea* is less fir-like, and the hooks are not as sharp. Unlike *Bonnemaisonia hamifera*, *Hypnea* is only found south of Cape Cod.

DATE

LOCATION

DATE

LOCATION

DATE

LOCATION

Algae

DULSE *Rhodymenia palmata*

Identification: This alga has a short stipe, which becomes mostly an expanded blade in an adult plant. The blade is flat and somewhat thick, with several divisions. As the blade extends upward from the round stalk, it widens, redivides, and then divides again. At the end, along the edge (or near the stalk of some plants), many unequal sections of new plants can be seen. Color: deep red purple. Size: to 1' (30cm).

Habitat: Found intertidally to subtidally.

Range: Arctic to Cape Cod.

Comments: This alga is harvested commercially both on the East Coast of North America and in Europe.

CRUSTOSE ALGAE *Lithothamnium* sp.

Identification: In contrast to the erect examples given in this book, this alga lies prostrate on rocks, other algae, and on shells. It may appear as a crust, a cushion, a stain, or a disk shape. A microscope is needed to determine the specific cell type. For some crustose algae, a drop of hydrochloric acid will cause fizzing. To determine individual species of this group of algae goes beyond the scope of this book. Color: greenish, pinkish reds and browns. Size: variable.

Habitat: Found on hard substrate, intertidally to subtidally.

Range: Arctic to Cape Cod.

Comments: These are some of the deepest-growing algae. They often thrive on the shells of gastropods.

EEL GRASS *Zostera marina*

Identification: This plant grows from a creeping runner that sends out grass-like blades at intervals. It bears inconspicuous flowers and fruits in late spring and early summer. Color: green; older leaves die and turn black. Size: leaves, 1/4" to 1/2" wide (6mm to 12mm) and up to 3' long (.9m).

Habitat: Grows in soft sediment, in shallow bays.

Range: Arctic to South Carolina.

Comments: Eel Grass is a true angiosperm in that it produces flowers and fruit, which marine algae do not. It is important ecologically because it provides shelter for small invertebrates and fish, and it stabilizes the sediments in shallow bays. Eel grass was formerly the sole food item for Brant Geese until a blight infected the beds in the 1920s and '30s. This reduced the population of this plant. At one time, eel grass was used as a stuffing material in mattresses and as insulation around shorefront houses.

DATE

LOCATION

DATE

LOCATION

DATE

LOCATION

PORIFERA (Sponges)

At one time, sponges were thought to be plants because they did not move or visibly capture food. This would imply that they photosynthesized their nourishment, which is not the case. Today we know that sponges are, indeed, animals because they carry on biological functions that are characteristic of animals. Individual cells of the sponge have become specialized for different functions and work together for the good of the whole animal. Some cells create the water current to bring in food; some cells take waste products out; some cells carry on digestion; some cells make spicules (structural stiffeners); and, some cells facilitate reproduction. Individual cells do not *carry out* all the biological functions, but they take care of all the needs of the sponge. This is called organization at the "cellular" level.

The phylum name Porifera means "pore bearer," and the typical sponge body plan has holes or pores on all surfaces. The pores enable the sponge to filter-feed by creating a current of water that is drawn through its body. Many small pores on the outside, called ostia (singular, ostium), bring water and food into the sponge. Specialized cells capture waterborne food as it passes through the sponge. A large central opening is called the osculum (there may be more than one) from which the water leaves the sponge. The constant movement of water through the animal brings in a supply of food and oxygen, and carries away waste products in the process.

The skeleton of a sponge provides a rigid support, or frame, for the body. It protects the animal from enemies, although only a few fish and sea stars will eat sponges. The skeleton is a combination of spongin and spicules. Spongin is a protein mass that surrounds and supports stiff, needle-like spicules. Spicules may be composed of silica or calcareous material. Sponges may be most reliably identified by dissolving the spongin and looking at the spicules with magnification. To do this, place a small piece of sponge on a glass dish. Apply a small amount of chlorine bleach and, in a very short time, the only part of the sponge that remains will be the spicules. Use a 10X hand lens or magnifying glass to see what type of spicules are present, and check with a biology text or identification key.

Calcareous Sponges—Spicules are needle shaped with three or four branches.

Glass Sponges—Spicules are made up of linked glass fibers that may have six rays, hooks, rods, or needles.

Siliceous/Horny Sponges—Spicules are needle shaped with four rays. Most sponges covered here are in this group.

Sponges may reproduce either by budding (asexual reproduction) or by means of eggs and sperm (sexual reproduction). In the sexual reproduction of some sponges, both eggs and sperm may originate from the same individual. In other species of sponges, the sexes are separate, and the aforementioned water current brings the sperm of one sponge to the sponge containing the eggs. The fertilized eggs develop into flagellated larvae that eventually escape from the parent sponge and swim away. After a short time, they settle down and attach to the substrate and develop into a new sponge.

Members of the phylum Porifera are marine, except for one family of freshwater sponges. In the tropics, some species—like the barrel sponges—can be large enough to hold a person; others—like the purple tube sponges—can be tubes and pillars taller than a person. Most sponges of the North Atlantic are much smaller in height and are seen as simple encrustations on rocks or as low, branching projections.

Spicule Terms:

Style—each end of the spicule is different

Strongylote—one end of the spicule is rounded

Strongyles—both ends are rounded

Oxeote—the pointed end of the spicule

Oxeas—spicules pointed at each end

Tylotes—both ends of the spicules are knobbed

Tylostyle— straight; rounded on one end and tapering to a point on the other

Sponge

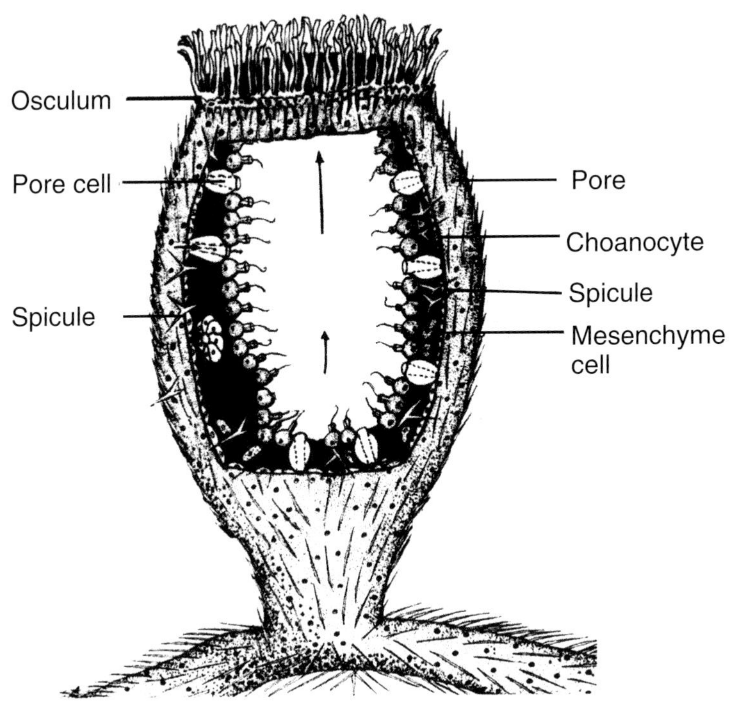

Spicules

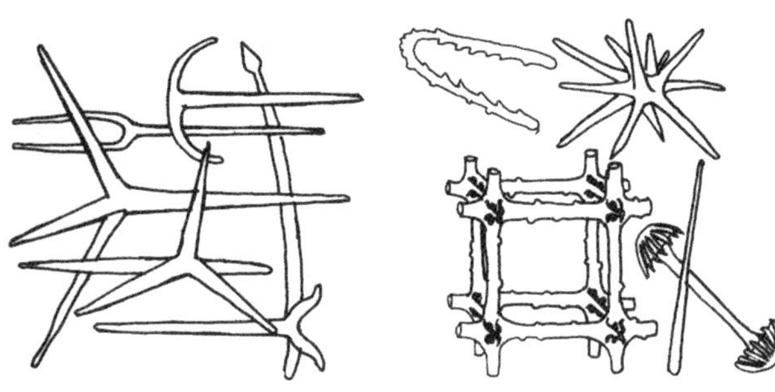

Spicules from calcareous sponges

Spicules from silicious sponges

Sponges

FINGER SPONGE *Haliclona oculata*

Identification: This sponge varies in its shape and in the number of its branches. It has a short stalk, and the oscula are conspicuous. Branches are somewhat flat on sponges north of Cape Cod and somewhat rounder on sponges to the south. Color: light brown to grayish-brown, sometimes purplish. Size: height, 18" (46cm); width, 12" (30cm).

Habitat: Found on rocks, from low tide line to 400' (124m).

Range: Labrador to North Carolina.

Comments: Also known as Eyed Sponge due to the large oscula on the branches. It is often found washed up on beaches after storms. Spicules have oxeas of different sizes.

CRUMB OF BREAD SPONGE *Halichondria panicea*

Identification: This common, encrusting sponge covers rocks and pilings with irregular masses. When it grows on the underside of rocks, it forms tab-like projections or cones with a conspicuous osculum. Color: yellow to greenish. Size: height, 2" (50mm); width, 2' (60cm).

Habitat: Found on the solid substrate, intertidally to 200' (61m).

Range: Arctic to Cape Cod.

Comments: The Crumb of Bread Sponge gets its name from its texture and the ease with which it breaks apart. The green color found in some specimens is due to the presence of a symbiotic, a microscopic algae called zoochlorellae. Spicules: oxeas with some strongyles.

The green color of this Crumb of Bread Sponge is due to the presence of zoochlorellae, a microscopic algae

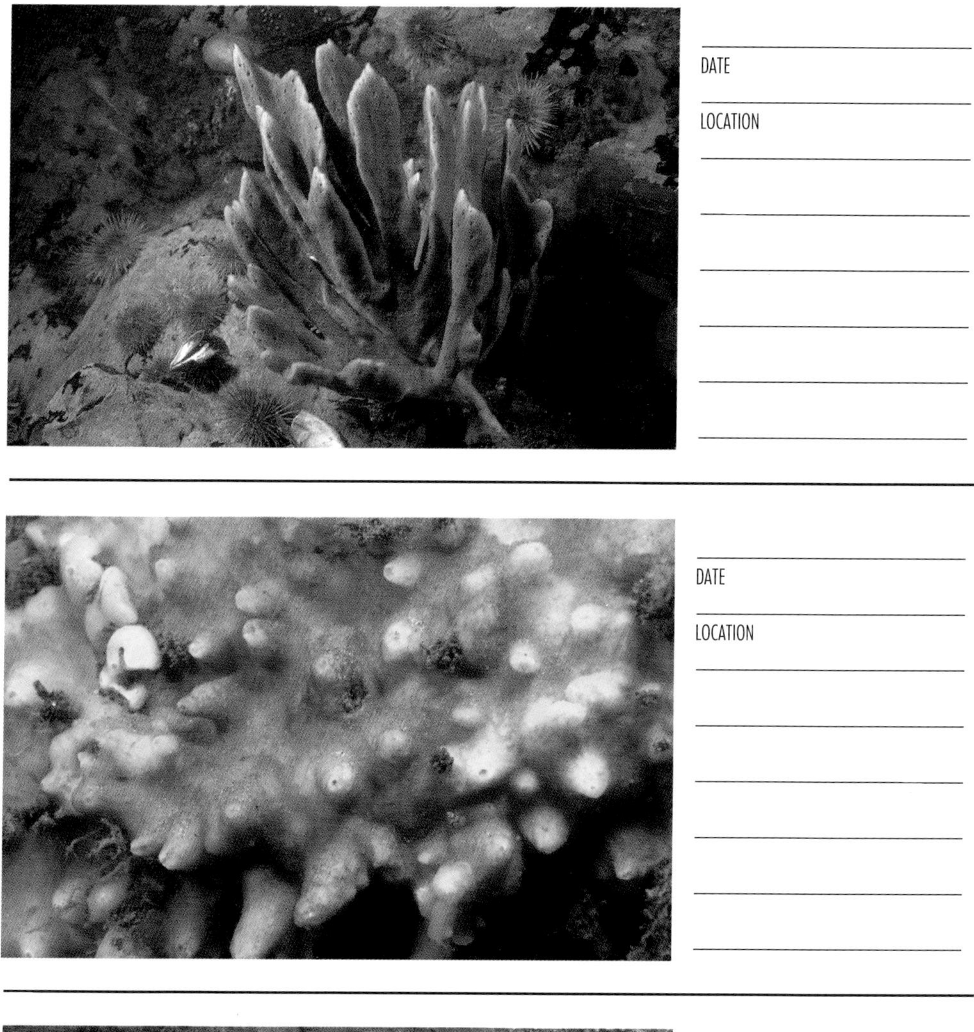

DATE

LOCATION

DATE

LOCATION

DATE

LOCATION

Sponges

PURPLE SPONGE *Haliclona permollis*

Identification: This common encrusting sponge is smooth and soft. It has 1/4" (6mm) oscula that are on raised tubes. Sometimes this sponge forms branches that may interconnect. Color: pink to purple. Size: height, 1⅝" (41mm); width, 3' (.9m).

Habitat: Found on hard substrate in protected waters, intertidally to 20' (6m).

Range: Gulf of St. Lawrence to Chesapeake Bay.

Comments: The Purple Sponge is still being studied and may be more than one species. Spicules: oxeas.

BORING SPONGE *Cliona celata*

Identification: This firm, textured sponge develops into irregular shapes that are covered with low, wartlike protrusions measuring about 1/16" to 3/16" in diameter. Color: sulphur yellow.

Habitat: Gravel and shell covered bottoms, subtidally to 100' (30m).

Range: Gulf of St. Lawrence to Gulf of Mexico.

Comments: The free-swimming larval stage may land on a mollusk shell and develop into a sponge there. As the animal grows, it secretes an acid that dissolves its host's shell. The Boring Sponge is considered a problem in oyster beds. Spicules: tylostyles.

RED BEARD SPONGE *Microciona prolifera*

Identification: In its early stages, this is an encrusting sponge; as it begins to increase in size, it forms lobes and eventually develops branches. Oscula are small and scattered over the surface of the sponge. Color: generally, orange to red. Size: up to 8" (20cm).

Habitat: Found on pilings, shells, and rocks, subtidally to moderate depth.

Range: Nova Scotia to Texas.

Comments: This hardy sponge can withstand pollution and the low salinities of bays and estuaries. Spicules: the largest are smooth styles and oxeas.

Similar Species: Palmate Sponges, *Isodictya* sp., are also reddish, but the osculas are large and conspicuous.

DATE

LOCATION

DATE

LOCATION

DATE

LOCATION

Sponges

COMMON PALMATE SPONGE *Isodictya palmata*

Identification: This sponge grows branches that are more flat than round. The oscula are easily visible along the sides of the branches. Color: yellow, orange, or light brown. Size: 12" (30cm) in height and width.

Habitat: Grows on solid substrate, subtidally to moderate depth.

Range: Nova Scotia to Cape Hatteras.

Comments: Often found on beaches after storms. Spicules: larger ones are oxeas and styles.

WARTY SPONGE *Melonanchora elliptica*

Identification: This massive, wart-like sponge often has projecting lobes on which its large oscula are located. The surface is covered with many small bumps. Color: yellowish. Size: 3' (1m).

Habitat: Found on rocks, pilings, and other hard substrate, from the low tide line to 150' (46m).

Range: Gulf of St. Lawrence to Caribbean.

Comments: This sponge often covers large rocks and has small arthropods living in its crevices.

CHALICE SPONGE *Phakellia ventilabrum*

Identification: This cup-shaped sponge often has a short, slender stalk. Like most sponges it is quite variable in form (younger sponges are often fan-shaped). The surface is smooth or somewhat ridged with small oscula. Color: yellow to tan. Size: height, 6" (15cm); width, 8" (20cm).

Habitat: Found on rocks, pilings, and other hard substrate.

Range: Gulf of St. Lawrence to Brazil.

Comments: Small crustaceans are often found in the cups.

DATE

LOCATION

DATE

LOCATION

DATE

LOCATION

CNIDARIA
(Coelenterates)

Cnidaria is a large and varied phylum that includes jellyfish, sea anemones, hydra, corals, and colonial hydroid medusae. Members of the phylum have reached the "tissue" level of organization, where cells act together as a unit to perform a common function. This is a distinct advantage for an animal. For example, nerve cells that are linked together are better able to pass information than single, unconnected nerve cells. Cnidarians have a digestive system that is connected to the outside through a mouth, which is also a feature of all the more evolved animals.

Cnidarians occur in both the polyp and medusa form. A typical polyp body plan is a tube that is radially symmetrical. It is attached to substrate at one end, while the other end forms a mouth that is encircled with tentacles. The mouth is the only opening to the gut. The tentacles are all armed with explosive stinging cells, called nematocysts, which react upon contact with zooplankton or small fish. A poison in the nematocyst kills or numbs the prey organism, and tentacles bring it into the mouth. A typical medusa has an umbrella-shaped body surrounded by tentacles for stinging and capturing prey. The mouth is located ventrally (in the center), with a long tube extending from it.

Many cnidarians have alternating polyp-medusa stages. The medusae release eggs and sperm that develop into planula larvae, the ovoid or pear shaped, free-swimming offspring of cnidarians. They are dispersed over long distances by coastal and ocean currents. The larvae settle on a suitable substrate and eventually form polyps. When the polyps mature, they release leafs of young medusae that eventually become free-swimming, bell-shaped adults.

In other cnidarians, one of these reproductive stages may be much reduced or absent. Polyps may reproduce asexually by budding, as in some anemones, and may occur either singly or as a colony.

The three primary classes of Cnidaria are as follows:

Class Hydrozoa includes all hydroids. Most hydroids are polyp colonies and have alternating polyp-medusa stages.

Class Scyphozoa includes all the large medusae (true jellyfishes). All are marine medusae and can be generally distinguished from hydrozoa jellies by their large size and the lack of a velum. The polyp stage is either lacking or is very small.

Class Anthozoa includes sea anemones and coral. They occur only as polyps and have no free-swimming medusan generation.

Sea Anemone

Tentacles
Mouth
Oral disk
Mesentery
Acontium
Pedal disk

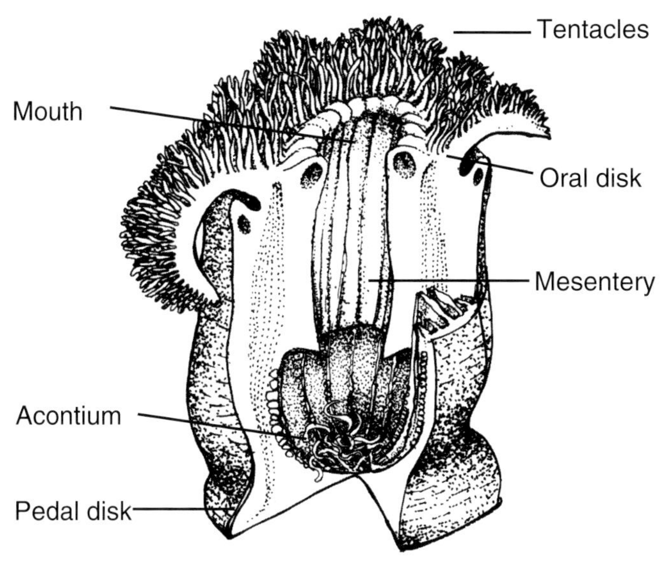

Hydromedusa cycle

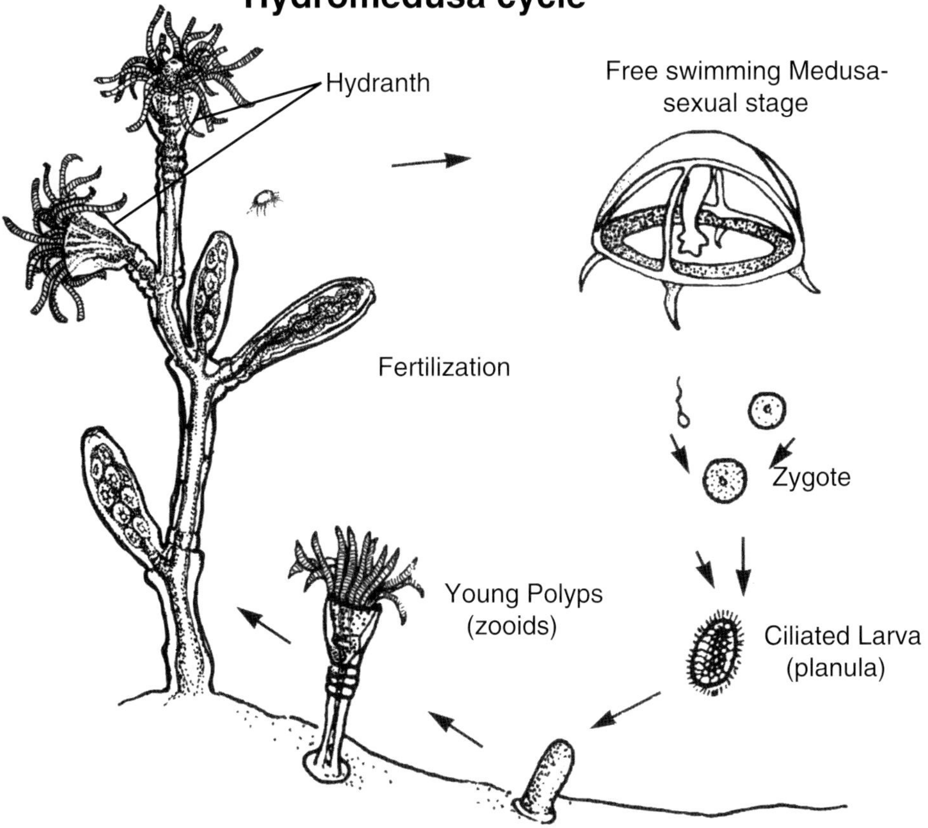

Hydranth
Free swimming Medusa-
sexual stage
Fertilization
Zygote
Young Polyps
(zooids)
Ciliated Larva
(planula)

Cnidarians/Hydrozoans

TUBULARIAN HYDROID *Tubularia crocea*

Identification: This common and beautiful hydroid is flower-like and grows in dense clumps with long, tangled stalks. There is one whorl of tentacles at the tip of the hydranth and a whorl of longer tentacles at the base of the hydranth. There are twenty to twenty-four tentacles in each whorl. The grape-like reproductive organs are near the base of the tentacles. Color: hydranths—red, pink, or white. Size: polyps—height, 5" (125mm); colony—width, 12" (30cm).

Habitat: Found on any hard object, subtidally (common on boat hulls).

Range: Nova Scotia to Florida.

Comments: The Tubularian Hydroid is a favorite food of the Red-Gilled Nudibranch, *Coryphella* sp., which is often found feeding on it. Also known as the Pink-Hearted Hydroid.

Tubularian Hydroid polyp at close hand

SOLITARY HYDROID *Hybocodon pendula*

Identification: The Solitary Hydroid has a column that is often imbedded in the sand and held in place by root-like structures. There is only one polyp on each column. It has thirty long, thin tentacles that surround the pear-shaped head and several rows of short tentacles located around the mouth. Color: whitish, with pinkish head. Size: height, 4" (102mm); width, 3/4" (19mm).

Habitat: Found on sand or mud, subtidally to 600' (182m).

Range: Arctic to Long Island, New York.

Comments: This beautiful hydroid is also able to feed by "bending over" and brushing its tentacles on the bottom. During April and May, the 1/4" medusa is very common near the coast. Also known as the One-Armed Jellyfish.

DATE

LOCATION

DATE

LOCATION

DATE

LOCATION

Cnidarians/Hydrozoans

CLAPPER HYDROMEDUSA *Sarsia tubulosa*

Identification: The feeding tube extends well past the elongated bell. Tentacles, feeding tubes, and canals can be white, blue, gold, or red. Size: Polyp colony is small—height, 3/4" (18mm); width, 4" (102mm). Medusa—height and width, 3/4" (18mm) .

Habitat: Polyps grow on rocks below the low-tide line. Medusae swim near the surface.

Range: Labrador to Chesapeake Bay.

Comments: Seen late spring to early summer.

SNAIL FUR *Hydractinia echinata*

Identification: This hydroid grows in colonies. Using magnification, one can see that they are composed of several types of hydroid individuals connected at the base by a stem. The polyps form a fuzz that is pink to orange. Size: to 3/16" (5mm).

Habitat: Found on snail shells containing hermit crabs.

Range: Subtidal in shallow water from Labrador to Florida.

Comments: It is believed that the stinging cells of the hydroids protect the hermit crab against some predators.

ZIG-ZAG WINE-GLASS HYDROID *Obelia geniculata*

Identification: The stems of this hydroid grow to about 1" without branching. Hydranths are conical, have twenty tentacles, and grow at alternating places on the stem. Hydrothecae are as wide as they are high, have no teeth, and stand out distinctly from the stem. Color: whitish. Size: colony—height, 1" (25mm); width, 12" (30cm).

Habitat: Found in shallow water on rocks, kelp, and other algae.

Range: Arctic to Florida.

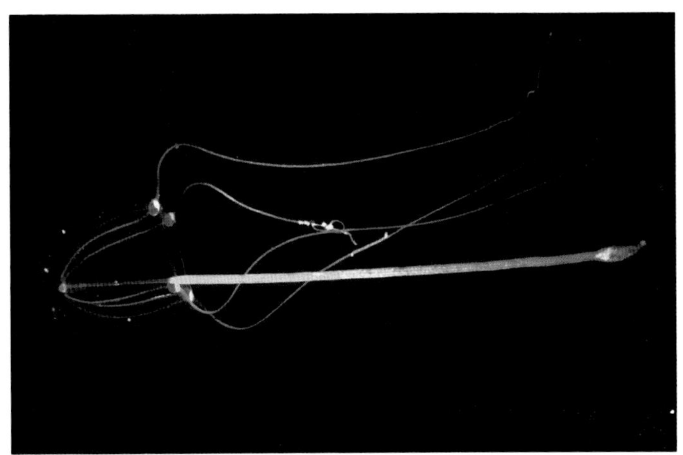

DATE

LOCATION

DATE

LOCATION

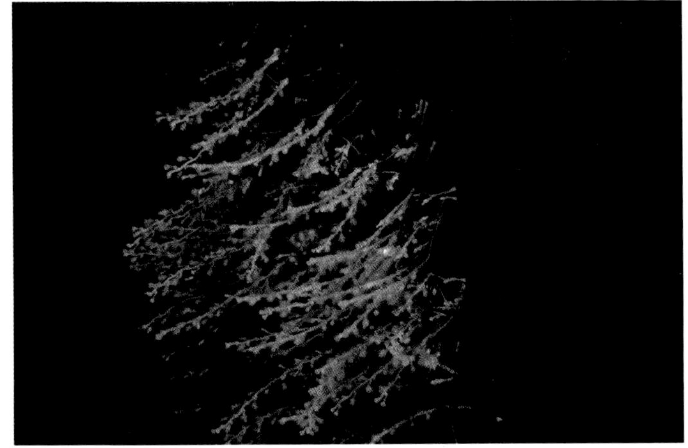

DATE

LOCATION

Cnidarians/Hydrozoans

LEPTOMEDUSA *Halopsis ocellata*

Identification: Leptomedusa typically has twelve to sixteen radial canals and wavy gonads. Its stomach is broad and flat. The mouth has four fairly short lips. There are up to four hundred and fifty small tentacles. Size: height, to 5/8" (16mm); width, to 2⅝" (65mm).

Habitat: Found along the coast but may also be oceanic.

Range: Greenland to New England and Northwestern Europe.

MANY-ARMED HYDROMEDUSA *Laodicae undulata*

Identification: The bell of this hydromedusa is somewhat flattened and has four hundred to six hundred tentacles whose tips are often coiled. The spiral cirri have club-shaped vesicles between them. There are long, sinuous gonads along the four radial canals. Color: transparent and white. Size: 1⅜" (34mm).

Habitat: Floats near surface along the coast.

Range: Massachusetts to West Indies.

Comments: Can be mistaken for the White-Cross Hydromedusa, *Staurophora mertensi,* since both seem to have a cross in the bell. *Laodicea undulata,* however, has spiral gonads on the cross.

MANY-RIBBED HYDROMEDUSA *Aequorea aequorea*

Identification: This hydromedusa has many radial canals (twenty-five to a hundred), the number increasing with age. When the animal is mature, there are two to three times as many tentacles and many more marginal vesicles. The bell is saucer-shaped and in some individuals reaches 7" (175 mm) in diameter. Polyp stage is unknown.

Habitat: Oceanic.

Range: Maine to Gulf of Mexico.

Similar species: *Rhacostoma atlanticum* has tiny bumps in rows on the underside of the bell.

Comments: Seen summer through fall.

DATE

LOCATION

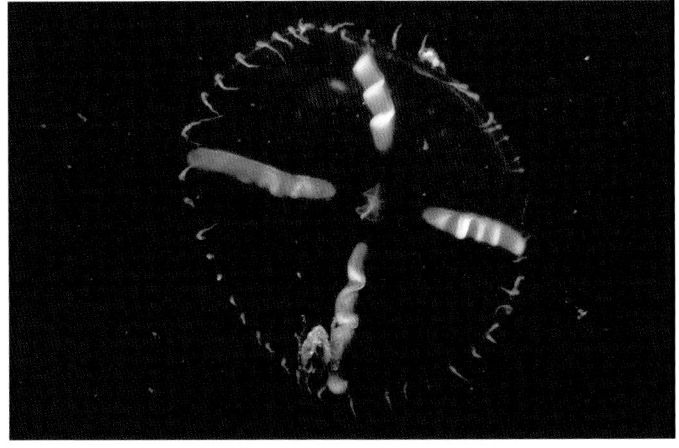

DATE

LOCATION

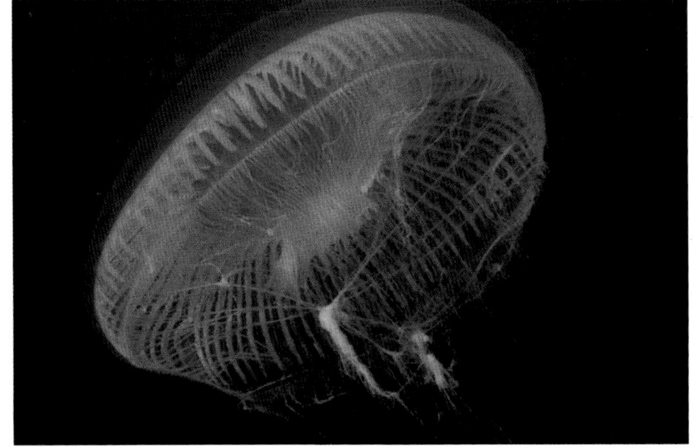

DATE

LOCATION

Cnidarians/Hydrozoans

WHITE CROSS HYDROMEDUSA *Staurophora mertensi*

Identification: This hydromedusa has four fringed radial canals that form a milky-white cross and a slit-like mouth that continues under each radial canal. The bell is flattened and has many tentacles. It can reach 12" (30cm) wide and 2" (48mm) high. Polyp stage is unknown.

Habitat: Found along the coast. At night it rises to just below the surface.

Range: Arctic to Rhode Island.

Comments: This medusa feeds on other medusae and crustaceans. In the northern part of its range, it is seen spring through late summer. In the southern range, it is normally found spring to early summer.

HYDROMEDUSA *Aequorea macrodactyla*

Identification: This hydromedusa has a thick, lens-shaped central disk and a thin margin. The stomach is half as wide as the medusa's umbrella, and there are usually sixty to a hundred (at times one hundred and fifty) radial canals. Tentacles: ten to thirty on which there are six to eight times as many small bulbs. Color: transparent and white. Size: to 3" (75mm).

Habitat: Mainly oceanic, but may come close to shore.

Range: Nearly worldwide.

Comments: May reproduce by fission or by going through a medusa-polyp cycle.

This medusa is dividing into three medusae

DATE

LOCATION

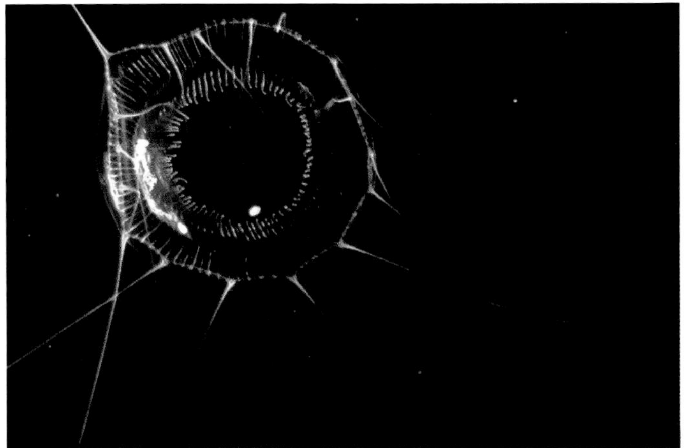

DATE

LOCATION

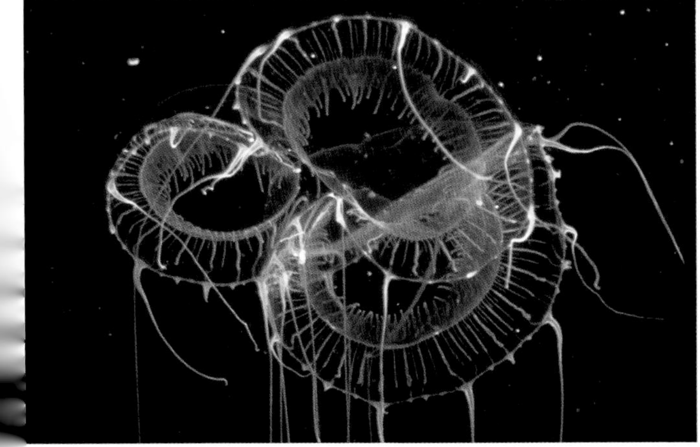

DATE

LOCATION

EIGHT-RIBBED HYDROMEDUSA *Melicertum octocostatum*

Identification: The medusa is bell-shaped and has eight radial canals. When mature, there are seventy-two long tentacles and seventy-two short tentacles along the bottom of the bell. Color: variations of gold or white; may be transparent. Size: to 3/4" (18mm) high and wide.

Habitat: Polyp stage is found on shells and rocks below the low-tide line. Medusa swims near the surface.

Range: Arctic to Cape Cod.

Comments: Seen spring through summer.

The Eight-ribbed Hydromedusa

ELEGANT HYDROMEDUSA *Tima formosa*

Identification: This beautiful hydromedusa is unmistakable when mature. In mature adults, the manubrium extends below the bell. It has thirty-two tentacles of three different lengths. The polyp is very small. Size: medusa—height, 2½" (62mm); width, 4" (102mm).

Habitat: Occasionally near shore.

Range: Arctic to Rhode Island.

Comments: North of Cape Cod, this medusa is found in the fall. On the Cape and southward, it is found all year.

DATE

LOCATION

DATE

LOCATION

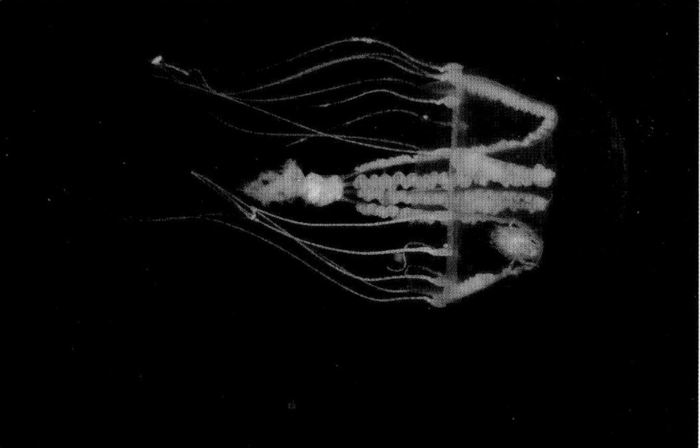

DATE

LOCATION

SIPHONOPHORE *Agalma elegans*

Identification: The anterior section is a transparent gas-filled float. It provides locomotion and regulates depth. The next section, armed with nematocyst cells (stinging cells used for capturing prey), is comprised of many tentacles that are up to 12" (30cm) long. When the colony is moving, these tentacles follow in a straight line, but when it is still and feeding, the strands spread in all directions. Size: anterior section—to 4" (102mm).

Habitat: Floats close to shore.

Range: Nova Scotia to Chesapeake Bay.

Comments: Each of these pelagic hydrozoan colonies is made up of different individuals, each performing a separate function such as reproduction, locomotion, flotation, or feeding. The most well known Siphonophore is the Portuguese Man-of-War.

Close-up of tentacles

Close-up of tentacles

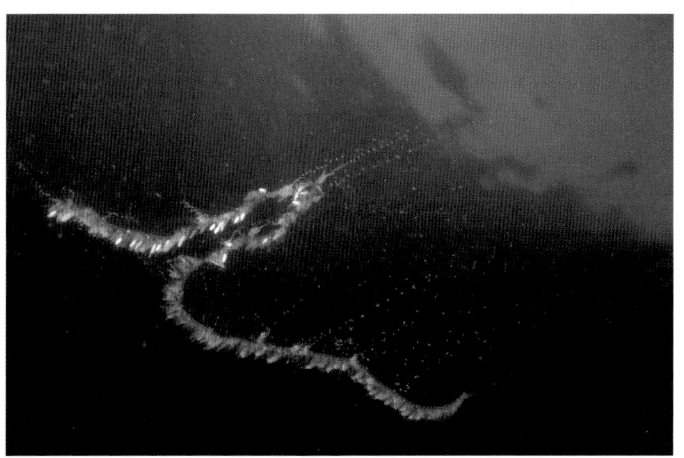

DATE

LOCATION

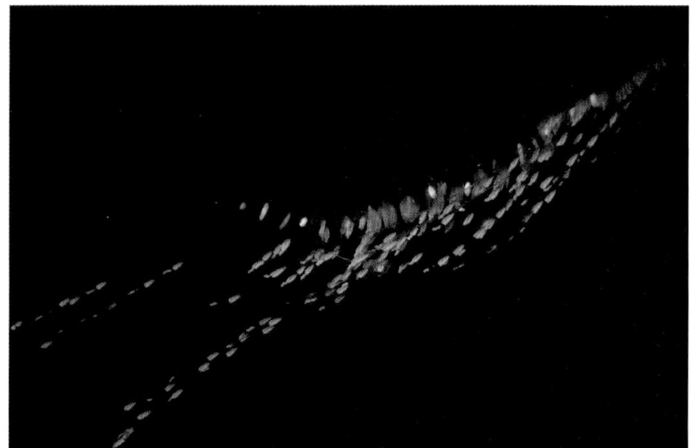

DATE

LOCATION

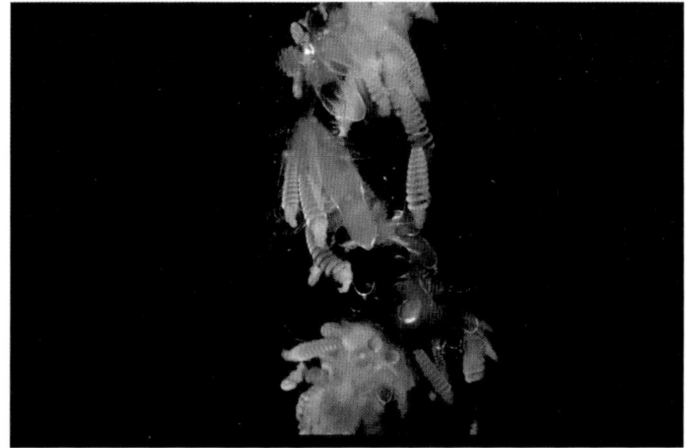

DATE

LOCATION

Cnidarians/Scyphozoans

LION'S MANE JELLY *Cyanea capillata*

Identification: This giant jellyfish has a saucer-shaped bell with many tentacles and mouth-arms. The umbrella margin has eight main lobes; each, in turn, is partially divided by a deep, median cleft with two notches on each side of it. The feeding tube is stout and extends greatly. Under the bell and on each side of the stomach, there are four highly-folded gonads. This creature's powerful muscular system allows it to move through the water with ease. Color: varies with age; bell is pink to brownish purple; stomach has a yellowish margin. The small Lion's Mane Jellies are pink, while the larger ones are more brown to purple. Size: to 8' (2.4m) in diameter.

Habitat: Found near the surface along the coast.

Range: Arctic to Florida.

Comments: Also known as the Red Jelly, this scyphozoan can grow to be the largest jellyfish in the world. It has been reported to be as large as 8' (2.4m) in diameter in its northern range, with tentacles as long as 200' (61m). Anyone who swims in the ocean during June and the first part of July needs to be aware of the high concentrations of young medusae during this time. This species is very toxic and can be fatal to swimmers.

MOON JELLY *Aurelia aurita*

Identification: This common jellyfish has four distinct horseshoe-shaped gonads. Tentacles are marginal, small, and numerous (at least 240). The sense organs lie between the margins of each of the eight lobes (octants). Color: whitish to translucent; gonads—white or yellow brown to pink. Size: to 16" (41cm).

Habitat: Found near the surface, close to shore.

Range: Arctic to Mexico.

Comments: The most common jellyfish that washes up on beaches. Its sting may cause a minor rash and itch for a few hours.

Remains of a Moon Jelly on the sand

Photo: Fred Bavendam

DATE

LOCATION

Photo: Fred Bavendam

DATE

LOCATION

DATE

LOCATION

STALKED JELLYFISH *Haliclystus auricula*

Identification: The Stalked Jellyfish does not look like other jellyfish since it has a plump stalk and its mouth faces upward. The bell is flower-shaped and is divided into eight lobes. Between the lobes are bundles of short, knobby tentacles that resemble pom-poms. At the base of each indentation, there is a pad-like adhesive organ that serves as an anchor when necessary. Color: variable—red, blue, green, orange, purple, and pink. Size: 1¼" (31mm).

Habitat: Found on rocks, eel grass, kelp, and other algaes, intertidally to shallow water.

Range: New Brunswick to Cape Cod.

Comments: The Stalked Jellyfish traps small worms and other invertebrates with its tentacles and puts them into its mouth. It matures in one season and disappears in the fall. Also known as the Eared-Stalked Jellyfish.

DEAD MAN'S FINGERS *Alcyonium siderium*

Identification: This soft coral grows fleshy lobes and fingers. The polyps resemble small anemones and have eight pinnate tentacles. Color: white to pale orange. Size: 4" to 8" (10cm to 20cm).

Habitat: Found in quiet waters on rocks and pilings, subtidally to 25' (7.5m).

Range: Gulf of St. Lawrence to Rhode Island.

Comments: All soft corals belong to the subclass Octocorallia and have eight tentacles.

The column of this soft coral contains embryos (small spheres) that are soon to be released

DATE

LOCATION

DATE

LOCATION

DATE

LOCATION

RED SOFT CORAL *Gersemia rubiformis*

Identification: This branching coral colony is soft and fleshy, with thick, pear-shaped clusters of lobes growing from one main stem. Except near the base, the stem is covered with red spicules. Color: red to orange. Size: height, 6" (15cm); width, 3" (75mm).

Habitat: Found on hard substrate, subtidally.

Range: Arctic to Gulf of Maine.

Red Soft Coral (close-up)

LINED ANEMONE *Fagesia lineata*

Identification: The column of this small anemone is slender and usually white to brownish. The oral disc is surrounded by forty thin tentacles arranged in three rings. Size: height, 1¼" (31mm); width, 1/4" (6mm).

Habitat: On and under rocks, subtidally to 65' (19.5m).

Range: Cape Cod to Cape Hatteras.

Comments: At times, this delicate anemone is found in great concentrations, presenting a beautiful sight.

DATE

LOCATION

DATE

LOCATION

DATE

LOCATION

NORTHERN STONY CORAL *Astrangia danae*

Identification: This stony coral is often found in colonies of up to thirty polyps that can have a circumference of 4" (100mm) to 5" (127mm). Polyp diameter is 1/4" (6mm). Color: off-white to pink, but animals that live in sunny areas can be translucent.

Habitat: Found on hard substrate, subtidally to 130' (28m).

Range: Cape Cod to Florida.

Comments: This is the only hard coral in our cool waters.

Northern Stony Coral with polyps retracted

SILVER-SPOTTED ANEMONE *Bunodactis stella*

Identification: This small anemone is wider than it is tall. The column has many rows of sticky lumps. The oral disk has six bright white lines radiating from the mouth. There are 120 slender, smooth tentacles, which often have a white line in the middle and a light spot at the base. The basal disk attaches the anemone to the hard substrate. Color: variable—bluish green, translucent, and reddish. Size: height, 1½" (38mm); width, 2" (51mm).

Habitat: Found on hard substrate, in shallow water.

Range: Nova Scotia to Gulf of Maine.

Comments: Because the anemone's column is so sticky, it is often covered with pebbles and bits of shell.

DATE

LOCATION

DATE

LOCATION

DATE

LOCATION

NORTHERN RED ANEMONE *Urticina felina*

Identification: The Northern Red is a large, stout, colorful anemone with a hundred thick tentacles in several rings around the mouth. The soft, broad column has many vertical rows of small suckers, to which small objects can attach. The column is flexible and changeable in shape. The tentacles can retract, and the column margin can be pulled in over the oral disk for protection. The mouth is in the center of the oral disk and can expand in order to accept food from the tentacles. The tentacles are armed with powerful nematocyst stinging cells. Color: variable—red, orange, yellow, white, or combinations of these. Size: height, 5" (127mm); width, 3" (76mm).

Habitat: Strongly adheres to rocks in protected places, from low tide line to over 100' (30m).

Range: Arctic to Cape Cod.

Comments: In the northern part of its range, the Northern Red is found in shallow water. Also known as *Tealia crassicornis* (and formerly known as *Tealia felina*). It feeds on many animals including small fish, urchins, crabs, and other invertebrates.

The mouth of the Northern Red Anemone (center right)

Color variations in Northern Red Anemones (left)

A Northern Red Anemone eating a Moon Jelly (bottom right)

DATE

LOCATION

DATE

LOCATION

DATE

LOCATION

Northern Red Anemones feeding on an egg veil (egg mass), perhaps that of a Goosefish

The "orange balls" inside the anemone are developing embryos that will be released from the tip of the tentacles

---

RED STOMPHIA *Stomphia coccinea*

Identification: The column is soft, smooth, and changeable in form (normally higher than wide, sometimes hour glass shaped). The basal disk is generally wider than the column. The oral disk is surrounded by ninety-six pale red, stout tentacles in three rows. The oral disk's shape is variable; it may be flat, convex, or concave. Color: column—red, pink, greenish, orange, mottled, or streaked irregularly; tentacles—two to three reddish bands. Size: height, 5" (127mm); width, 3" (75mm).

Habitat: Found on rocks, from low tide line to 150' (46m).

Range: Gulf of St. Lawrence to Cape Cod.

Similar Species: Laboratory study may be necessary to confirm that this is a true species rather than a variety of the Northern Red Anemone, *Urticina felina.* However, Red Stomphia, *Stomphia coccinea,* does not have rows of small suckers on the main column as does the Northern Red Anemone.

DATE

LOCATION

DATE

LOCATION

DATE

LOCATION

FRILLED ANEMONE *Metridium senile*

Identification: This common anemone has a tall, smooth column with a widely expanded oral disk. The disk is divided into waved lobes and is surrounded by many small, slender tentacles (a thousand in adults) that do not have color rings. The multitude of tentacles creates a frilled appearance. Color: variable; column—brownish, white, cream colored, or mottled; tentacles—whitish. Size: height, 18" (46cm); width, 9" (23cm).

Habitat: Found on solid substrate, intertidally to 150' (45.5m).

Range: Arctic to Delaware.

Comments: The Frilled Anemone can reproduce both asexually and sexually. In asexual reproduction, it may split longitudinally (fission) and create a new individual. Or, it may slough off small fragments from its base (pedal laceration) to make new "little anemones." It reproduces sexually in the usual way: eggs are fertilized by sperm, creating free-swimming larvae. This anemone has powerful stinging cells on thread-like strands, called acontia, that it can use to defend itself when greatly stressed. The Maned Nudibranch, *Aeolidia papillosa,* is one of its predators.

The mouth of the Frilled Anemone

A Frilled Anemone releasing eggs into the water

DATE

LOCATION

DATE

LOCATION

DATE

LOCATION

The small anemones at the base of the Frilled Anemone are produced asexually by means of a process called pedal laceration

Frilled Anemones with their tentacles retracted

GHOST ANEMONE *Diadumene leucolena*

Identification: This small anemone is rather nondescript. The column appears generally smooth but has small, scattered bumps. Forty to sixty thin, pale, 1/2" (12mm) tentacles surround the mouth. Color: translucent, tinged with white, pink, or olive. Size: height, 1½" (38 mm); width, 1/2" (12.5 mm).

Habitat: Subtidally to shallow water. Found on or under rocks, pilings, and other hard substrate in protected waters, or in tide pools.

Range: Maine to North Carolina.

Comments: The Ghost Anemone looks similar to a young Frilled Anemone, *Metridium senile.*

DATE

LOCATION

DATE

LOCATION

DATE

LOCATION

RUGOSE (KNOBBY) ANEMONE *Hormathia nodosa*

Identification: The column of this distinct anemone is irregularly covered with low, roundish lumps. There are many tentacles around the mouth; those nearest the mouth are longer than those farther away. Color: oral disk—yellowish to tan; column—yellowish. Size: height, 5" (127mm); width, 2½" (63mm).

Habitat: Found on rocks, from 30' (9m) to deeper water.

Range: Gulf of St. Lawrence to Maine.

Comments: This beautiful anemone is often found near the Northern Red Anemone, *Urticina felina,* but at greater depths.

Rugose (Knobby) Anemones (the one on the right has tentacles retracted)

BURROWING ANEMONE *Edwardsia* sp. (probably *sipunculoides)*

Identification: Edwardsia anemones are small, slender, solitary animals that burrow into the sand with their tapering foot. Usually, the only visible part of the animal is the oral disk and tentacles, which can be seen on the surface of the sand. The number of tentacles varies from fourteen to thirty-six. Color: body—brown; oral disk and tentacles—white to tan. Size: height, 4" (96mm); width, 1" (24mm).

Habitat: Found in sandy or gravel bottoms.

Range: Arctic to Cape Cod.

NORTHERN CERIANTHID *Cerianthus borealis*

Identification: The Northern Cerianthid has two whorls of tentacles around the mouth. Those of the inner whorl are short, while the length of the outer tentacles varies from individual to individual. Color: body—brownish; oral disk—pale yellow brown, but darker toward the mouth. Size: height, to 18" (46cm); width, 1½" (38mm).

Habitat: Found in sand and mud, from 20' (6m) to 1600' (485m).

Range: Arctic to Cape Cod.

Comments: The Northern Cerianthid lacks a pedal disk. Such an organ is not necessary since this animal does not adhere to rocks but, instead, buries itself in sand or mud. The only parts of the animal that are usually visible are the oral disk, the tentacles, and a small section of the column.

DATE

LOCATION

DATE

LOCATION

DATE

LOCATION

CTENOPHORA
(Comb Jellies)

Ctenophora is a phylum of nearly transparent, fragile marine animals that float in the surface waters of the coast. Their body composition is 95 percent water by weight. Their varied body shapes can be described as round, oval, spherical, berry-like, or nut-like. They have specialized tissues but lack the true organs of more highly developed organisms.

Comb jellies have eight rows of external plates resembling a comb—hence their name. These plates are made of fused cilia. It is by the motion of the eight rows of cilia that they are able to move gently through the water. They are weak swimmers and are carried more by currents and tides than by their own efforts. During storms, they are often washed up on the shore and are a common sight for beachcombers.

Comb jellies are predators of marine plankton and feed mostly on other comb jellies, eggs, copepods, or fish larvae. When they swarm in large numbers, they can practically eliminate other planktonic life in that area. In representatives that have them, tentacles do not contain nematocysts (stinging cells) but, instead, have a sticky substance to which the prey adheres.

Ctenophores are hermaphroditic. Eggs and sperm are usually shed through the mouth to the exterior, and fertilization takes place in the water column. Larvae are planktonic except in the few species that brood their eggs. Comb jellies are known for their beautiful displays of color. The plates of fused cilia beat rapidly, refracting the light and producing dazzling colors. They also have phosphorescent cells in the body, adding to their beauty. For a diver, seeing a comb jelly underwater for the first time is truly a memorable event.

RHYNCHOCOELA
(Nemertean Worms)

Most nemertean worms are long, slender, and somewhat flattened. They have a mouth located ventrally, an inconspicuous anus located posteriorly, and a vascular system. Some may have eye spots. They are soft bodied and elastic. Their size ranges from under an inch to several feet.

Nemerteans would seem to be vulnerable because of their soft bodies; but, instead, they are carnivorous predators, paralyzing their prey with a venom. They have a sheathed, eversible proboscis that can be thrust out to almost the length of their body. They eat small crustaceans and annelid (segmented) worms. Color is the primary key when determining the species of nemerteans; therefore, worms must be kept alive for identification. Many are very colorful—red, orange, yellow, or green—and some have patterns of stripes or spots on top, with a pale underside.

Sexes are separate in most nemerteans. In most species, fertilization is external. Some species release eggs and sperm into the water, while others deposit eggs in masses of mucus. Eggs that are fertilized in the water column develop into larvae, swim about for a short period, then settle to become a small adult form. Eggs that are deposited in mucus develop into miniature adults. Some nemerteans reproduce asexually by regeneration, where pieces of themselves become new individuals.

BRYOZOA
(Moss Animals)

Resembling seaweeds, delicate coral, embroidered cloth, or colonial hydroids, bryozoans tend to be overlooked by the average diver or beachcomber. The name reflects the plant-like appearance of these sedentary, colonial animals. Individuals are rarely as big as 1/32" (1mm), while colonies may grow to 1' (30cm). The representatives of this phylum are mostly marine, but there are some freshwater species.

More than four thousand species are included in the bryozoan phylum. The individual protective container is called a zooecia, while the animal inside is called a zooid. All species have a circle of tentacles, called lophophores, around the mouth. Species are differentiated by the size and shape of the mouth opening as well as by the presence or absence of tooth-like projections. The mouth and anus curve in a U-shape so that both are close together.

Bryozoan colonies can be calcareous or noncalcareous. They can grow into a variety of shapes. Large colonies of certain species may be plume-like, tufted, or branched like strands of seaweed. Other species may be more carpet-like, spreading over rocks, blades of algae, or mollusk shells. Colors can be as bright as brick red, or as inconspicuous as white to yellow beige.

The growth of a bryozoan colony is achieved by asexual budding. New colonies are created through sexual reproduction by the hermaphroditic individuals. Ciliated larvae, produced by the union of sperm and eggs, are free-swimming and eventually settle on the substrate.

Inspected with a 10X magnifier, bryozoans can provide interesting and provocative discoveries for the local beachcomber or diver.

BRACHIOPODA
(Lamp Shells)

All brachiopods are marine animals. The brachiopod shell is similar to a clam shell in that it has two valves. Because of this overt similarity, Phylum Brachiopoda was not separated from Phylum Molluska until the middle of the nineteenth century. The essential difference lies in the connection of the two valves. In mollusks, the shell is hinged laterally, which means the valves are on the right and left of the clam. In brachiopods, the valves are dorsal and ventral, which means the valves are on the top and bottom. This group also has a stalk-like, flexible pedicel which attaches the ventral valve to the substrate. Brachiopods have a row of tentacles with cilia, which drive water over them and trap food particles. They have separate sexes and, for most species, fertilization takes place in the water column.

The name "Lamp Shell" has been given to these animals because the shape of many brachiopods resembles that of ancient Roman oil lamps.

Ctenophores

SEA GOOSEBERRY *Pleurobrachia pileus*

Identification: The body of this ctenophore is egg-shaped with two long tentacles that are contractile; each is fringed on one side and can extend to a length twenty times that of the body. The body has eight rows of equally-spaced, comb-like ciliary plates that can extend to nearly the full length of the body. Color: transparent with iridescent ciliary plates. Size: height, 1⅛" (28mm); width, 1" (25mm).

Habitat: Near the shore.

Range: Nova Scotia to Florida.

Comments: Unlike jellyfish, Sea Gooseberries cannot sting. When in large groups, these active and voracious predators can clean an area of fish and invertebrate larvae. Their tentacles catch the prey by adhesion, then contract and place the food in the mouth.

COMMON NORTHERN COMB JELLY *Bolinopsis infundibulum*

Identification: The body of this ctenophore is oval and somewhat flat. It has two lobes that are less than half of the body length. There are four finger-like appendages at the mouth and eight rows of comb-like ciliary plates. Color: transparent with iridescent ciliary plates. Size: length, 6" (15cm); width, 2" (51mm).

Habitat: Along the coast.

Range: Arctic to Cape Cod, principally in the summer; Gulf of Maine, April to September.

Comments: This is the most common comb jelly in New England.

LEIDY'S COMB JELLY *Mnemiopsis leidyi*

Identification: The body of this large ctenophore is pear-shaped and almost colorless. The lobes are longer than the body. The ciliary plates are brightly luminescent and green when disturbed. Size: to 4" (102mm).

Habitat: Found in shallow water in bays and estuaries.

Range: Cape Cod Bay south to the Carolinas.

Comments: The lobes of the Northern Comb Jelly, *Bolinopsis infundibulum,* are shorter than its body, whereas the lobes of Leidy's Comb Jelly are longer than its body. At times, the young of a burrowing anemone, *Edwardsia leidyi,* are parasitic and are found in the gut of Leidy's Comb Jelly. The worm bores through the side of the comb jelly when it enters and, finally, leaves. The walls of the comb jelly then heal.

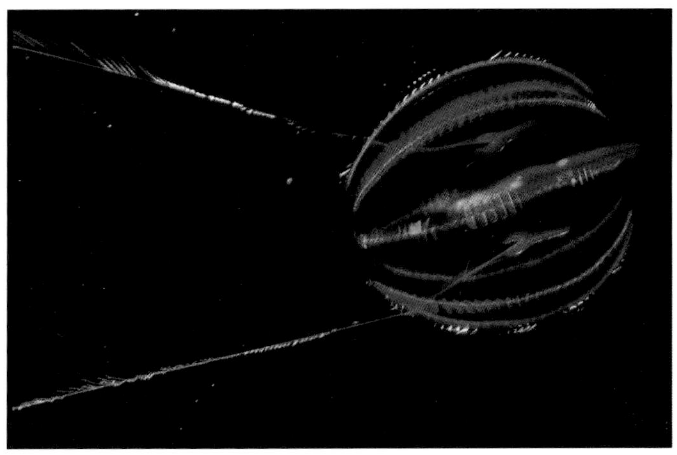

DATE

LOCATION

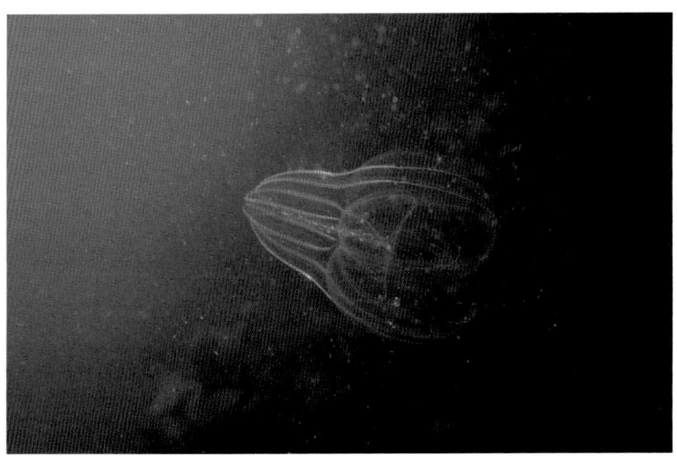

DATE

LOCATION

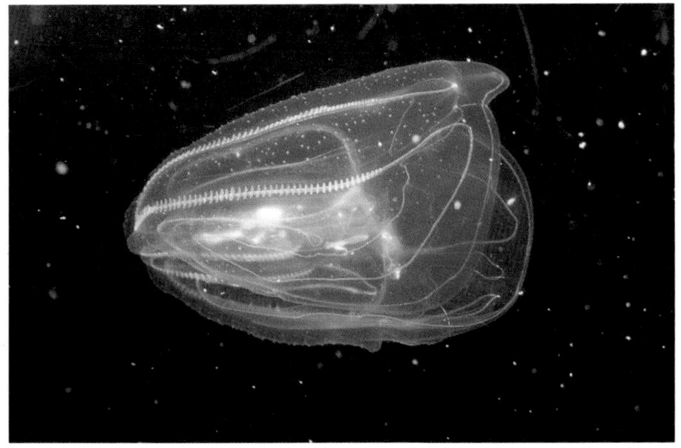

DATE

LOCATION

Ctenophores/Nemerteans/Bryozoans

BEROE'S COMMON JELLY *Beroe* sp.

Identification: The body of this comb jelly is sac-like and compressed laterally. There are no tentacles or lobes at any of its life stages. As in other ctenophores, there are eight rows of ciliary plates that run almost the complete length of the body. Color: translucent, rust, or pinkish, with iridescent ciliary plates. Size: length, 4½" (114 mm); width, 2" (50 mm).

Habitat: Found near shore.

Range: New Brunswick to Chesapeake Bay.

Comments: There are two species, B. *cucumis* in the northern part of the given range, and B. *ovata* in the southern part. Feeds mainly on cnidarian medusae and other comb jellies.

CHEVRON AMPHIPORUS *Amphiporus angulatus*

Identification: This worm has a white chevron behind the head and four groups of twelve to twenty eye spots (ocelli). Color: various shades of brown to purple. Size: length, 6" (15cm); width, 3/8" (9mm).

Habitat: Found in sand and in mud, subtidally to 450' (140m).

Range: Gulf of St. Lawrence to Cape Cod.

SEA LACE *Membranipora membranacea*

Identification: The colonies of this bryozoan are lacy crusts of irregular shapes. The zooids are rectangular with a membranous frontal wall. The colonies spread several inches over a variety of substrata. Color: white. Size: height, 1/32" (1mm); width, 3" (76mm).

Habitat: Found growing on almost everything from algae to hard substrate, from the low tide line to shallow water.

Range: Massachusetts to Long Island.

Comments: This bryozoan is common on kelp, where it grows both on the stipe and the blades. Also known as Lacy Crust.

DATE

LOCATION

DATE

LOCATION

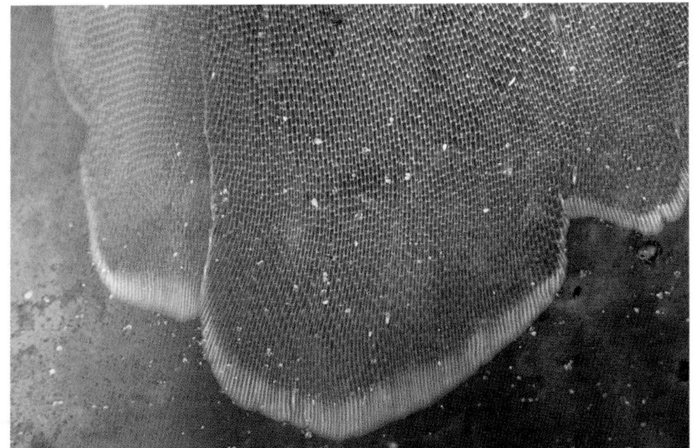

DATE

LOCATION

Bryozoans/Brachiopods

RED CRUST *Cryptosula pallasiana*

Identification: This encrusting colonial bryozoan is hard, thin, and irregularly shaped. The opening of the zooid is keyhole shaped. Color: orange to red, or purple brown. Size: colony—height, 1/32" (1mm); width, 3" (76mm).

Habitat: Found on rocks, shells, and algae; intertidally to shallow water.

Range: Nova Scotia to Florida.

Comments: Red Crust grows on several species of algae.

SPIRAL TUFTED BRYOZOAN *Bugula turrita*

Identification: The main branch of this beautiful, bushy, thickly tufted, erect bryozoan colony has secondary branches that spiral around it. Color: light yellow, orange, or tan. Size: height to 1' (30cm); width to 6" (15cm).

Habitat: Epiphytic on eel grass and algae, also found on rocks and pilings, from low tide line to 90' (27m).

Range: Bay of Fundy to Florida.

Comments: Very common, especially from Casco Bay, Maine, to North Carolina.

NORTHERN LAMP SHELL *Terebratulina septentrionalis*

Identification: The valves in this species are thin and pear-shaped, with many fine, radiating grooves. The lower valve is larger and has a notched beak. The hole in the beak allows the short pedicel (stem) to pass through and attach to rocks. Color: yellowish white. Size: length, 1¼" (31mm); width, 7/8" (22mm).

Habitat: Found intertidally to 12,500' (3810m).

Range: Labrador to New Jersey.

Comments: Superficially, the Northern Lamp Shell (and other braciopods) appears to be a bivalve mollusk, but it is connected dorsally and ventrally—not laterally, as are mollusks. Its name is derived from the fact that it looks like a Roman lamp.

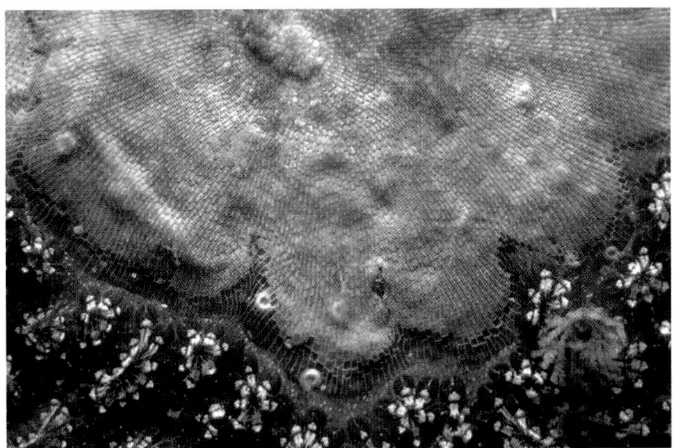

DATE

LOCATION

DATE

LOCATION

MOLLUSCA

This phylum represents one of the most popular groups of marine animals among humans, who use them in many different and varied ways. Except for Arthropoda, this is the largest invertebrate phylum, with over 100,000 species. The name Mollusca means "soft bodied." Representatives are found in both fresh and salt water, and on land.

There are four primary divisions (classes) of mollusks noted in this book: Polyplacophora (chitons), Gastropoda (snails), Bivalvia (bivalves), and Cephalopoda (squid and octopuses). All mollusks are built on the same fundamental plan, even though a clam appears to have little structural similarity to squid or snails. Representatives of this phylum have a thickened muscular mass of tissue (the foot) upon which the animal creeps or moves; a cloak-like covering (the mantle) that completely covers the animal and is responsible for secreting its shell of calcium; and a rasping tongue, called a radula, which is used for feeding. The molluscan radula is a belt of curved, chitinous teeth that are stretched over a cartilage base. The animals' rasping activities can range from a periwinkle grazing on algae to a moon snail drilling a hole in another gastropod's shell.

The anatomy is the same among these "soft bodied" animals, but it is different from that of other invertebrates. Mollusca have a heart that pumps the blood through extensively branched blood vessels and back again. They have a digestive system and a nervous system. Some mollusks are hermaphroditic (nudibranchs), and some have separate sexes (squid octopuses, and some gastropods), with a pair of gonads in the visceral mass. The larval stage is called a veliger larva.

From the Arctic to New England, variations in ocean temperature are responsible for molluscan distribution and for defining several distinct marine regions. One of these is the Arctic region, dominated by the Labrador current, which causes mollusks to be distributed wherever these cold waters travel along our northern coast. Another is the Boreal region, which encompasses an area from the Gulf of St. Lawrence to Cape Cod. The last is the Atlantic Region, which covers an area from Cape Cod to Florida, with both Cape Hatteras and Cape Cod representing geographic barriers for certain molluscan species.

Gastropod

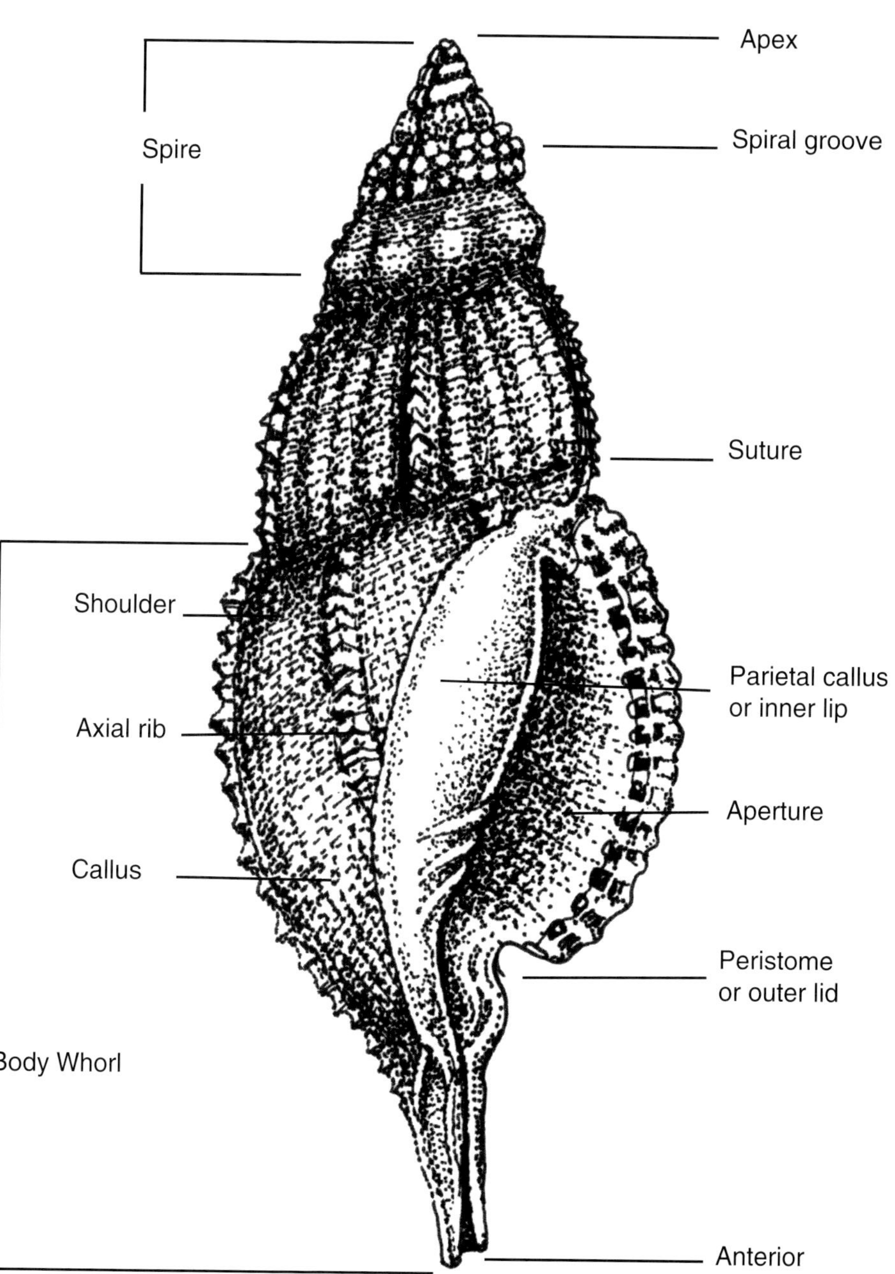
Apex
Spire
Spiral groove
Suture
Shoulder
Parietal callus
or inner lip
Axial rib
Aperture
Callus
Peristome
or outer lid
Body Whorl
Anterior

MOTTLED RED CHITON *Tonicella marmorea*

Identification: The eight valves of this chiton are dull, and the girdle (mantle) is smooth and leathery, without scales or hairs. There are twenty-five gills on each side of the foot. Color: variable—mottled, reddish, brown, bluish, green, and purple. Size: length, 1½" (37mm); width, 3/4" (18mm).

Habitat: Found on rocks and other hard substrate, low tide line to 300' (91m).

Range: Arctic to Massachusetts Bay.

Comments: This chiton is able to clamp firmly onto rocks by using its foot. It feeds on algae and many sessile animals such as sponges, hydroids, and bryozoans.

DRESSED CHITON *Amicula vestita*

Identification: The valves of this chiton are nearly covered by the girdle and its hair-like projections, leaving visible only a series of heart-shaped areas on the valves. Color: valves—gray, girdle—brown. Size: 2" (51mm).

Habitat: Found on rocks and other hard substrate, 30' (9m) to 180' (55m).

Range: Greenland to Cape Cod.

Comments: This chiton is actually quite common, but it is often overlooked because its cryptic coloration makes it difficult to see. Feeds on same animals as the Mottled Red Chiton.

TORTOISESHELL LIMPET *Acmaea testudinalis*

Identification: This small, oval, cone shell is hat-like, with an apex that is somewhat central. The outside of the shell can be checkered or have lines radiating from the apex. The markings along the inside border of the shell are checkered brown, black, or bluish white. Inside the shell, there is a dark brown patch near the center of the apex. Size: to 1" (25mm).

Habitat: Rocky shores, intertidally to subtidally.

Range: Arctic to Long Island.

Comments: The only common limpet found along the New England Atlantic coast. This animal is a herbivore.

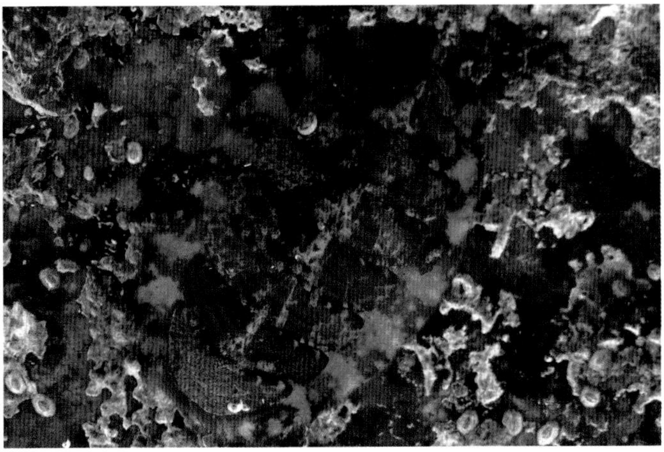

DATE

LOCATION

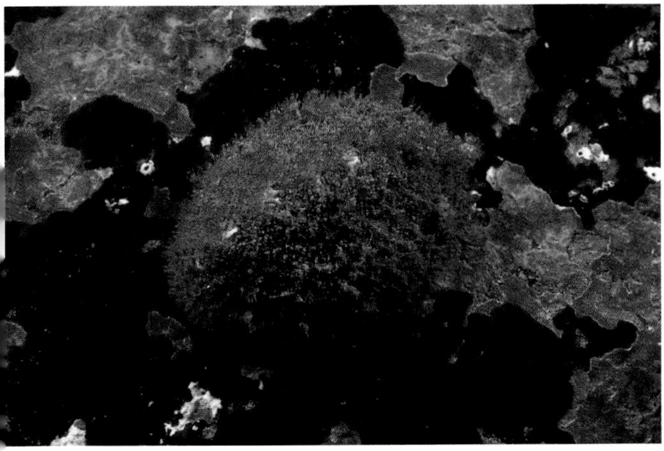

DATE

LOCATION

DATE

LOCATION

COMMON PERIWINKLE *Littorina littorea*

Identification: A thick, smooth, small snail of the littoral zone. Whitish columella continue along the inner edge of the shell's outer tip. The apex is blunt to eroded. Color: variable—dark gray to chocolate brown. Size: to 1" (25mm).

Habitat: Usually seen on algae, specifically *Ascophyllum nodosum* and *Fucus* species, as well as on algal films that cover rocks. Intertidal.

Range: Labrador to the south side of Chesapeake Bay.

Comments: This herbivore can be easily observed on rocky shores at low tide. It releases fertilized eggs into the water. This edible "winkle" was a European immigrant but is now so fully entrenched along our North Atlantic shore that it is considered quite common in its range.

ROUGH PERIWINKLE *Littorina saxatilis*

Identification: Smaller than the Common Periwinkle with a taller spire, the Rough Periwinkle has an ovate shell with distinct sutures and four to five convex whorls. The apex is pointed. Color: yellow to gray. Size: 1/2" (13mm).

Habitat: Found farther up in the intertidal zone than the Common or Smooth Periwinkle. Most often found on and under rocks near the blue-green algae (black) zone of rocky shores.

Range: Arctic to New Jersey.

Comments: Females of this species give birth to live, shelled young instead of aquatic eggs and larvae. This herbivorous species moves out to deeper water during winter and, thus, avoids the destructive abrasive action of ice.

SMOOTH PERIWINKLE *Littorina obtusata*

Identification: This small gastropod is round with a low spire. It has four whorls, the last of which is the largest. The aperture is round. Color: varies greatly—usually brownish yellow or orange yellow, but can be green, black, or brown. The Smooth Periwinkle can also have white or brown spiral bands. Size: 1/2" (12mm).

Habitat: Found on rockweed (*Fucus*) and knotted wrack (*Ascophyllum nodosum*), intertidally in the brown algal zone.

Range: Arctic to New Jersey.

Comments: This herbivorous gastropod is also known as Northern Yellow Periwinkle. It lays its egg masses directly on brown algae. Former scientific names were *Littorina palliata* (1822), *L. peconica* (1860), *L. littoralis* (1758) and *L. arctica* (1842).

DATE

LOCATION

DATE

LOCATION

DATE

LOCATION

BROWN-BANDED WENTLETRAP *Epitonium rupicola*

Identification: The shell is elongated and stout, tapering regularly to a pointed apex. There are ten rounded whorls, which have ten to sixteen fine ribs. The sutures are well defined. The aperture is nearly round with a white outer lip. Color: yellowish white with brownish bands. Size: height, 1" (25mm); width, 1/2" (12.5mm).

Habitat: Found in sand, from low-tide line to 120' (37m).

Range: Massachusetts to Texas.

Comments: Also known as Lined Wentletrap, this common gastropod releases a purple dye when irritated. Formerly named *E. lineatum*. Feeds on small anemones.

GREENLAND WENTLETRAP *Epitonium greenlandicum*

Identification: The shell is elongated and tapers regularly to a smooth apex. It has eleven to twelve convex whorls separated by deep wide sutures. The areas between the ribs are barred with close, revolving ridges. Color: spire—brownish, ribs—white. Size: length, 2" (51mm); width, 5/8" (16mm).

Habitat: Found on rock, mud, or sand from 60' to 600' (18m to 182m); has also been found as shallow as 30' (9.1m) in the northern part of its range.

Range: Arctic to Long Island, New York.

Comments: This is one of the most attractive shells in the north Atlantic.

Greenland Wentletrap extending its proboscis into a Frilled Anemone

DATE

LOCATION

DATE

LOCATION

DATE

LOCATION

COMMON SLIPPER SHELL *Crepidula fornicata*

Identification: The shell is convexed with a coiled apex turned down to one side. Because its shape is determined by the object to which it is attached, some shells are rather flat. Color: interior—white with brown markings, exterior—whitish with brown markings. Size: to 1½" (37mm). The interior shelf extends up to half the length of the shell.

Habitat: Found intertidally to 40' (12m) on the hard substrate; often seen on the carapace of horseshoe crabs. It is found where there is a high level of plankton.

Range: Canada to Texas.

Comments: Also known as the Atlantic Slipper Shell, Boat Shell, and Quarterdeck. These gastropods are often found in stacks where the bottom shell is the female and the top one is the male. The shells in the middle have undergone a sex change and are hermaphrodites. They are, therefore, able to fertilize each other. These shells are quite prolific. They grow on everything and have become a nuisance to boat owners.

Several Common Slipper Shells "stacked up" and undergoing sex reversal. The shell on the bottom is female, and the shell on top is male. Between the female and male are hermaphrodites.

FLAT SLIPPER SHELL *Crepidula plana*

Identification: The shell is flat or slightly curved. Its shape is often determined by the object to which it is attached. The apex is centrally located on the rear margin. The interior shelf is almost half the length of the shell. Color: white on the outside, glossy white on the inside. Size: to 1½" (37mm).

Habitat: Found on rocks and shells, intertidally. Also inside larger shells.

Range: Nova Scotia to Florida.

Comments: Also called Eastern White Slipper Shell.

DATE

LOCATION

DATE

LOCATION

DATE

LOCATION

NORTHERN MOON SNAIL *Lunatia heros*

Identification: The shell is thick and globular with five convex whorls. The spire is low. The aperture is large and oval with a whitish interior. The operculum is brown, thin, and horny. The umbilicus is open, showing the inside wall of the whorls almost to the apex. The foot is very large and gray. The tentacles are yellow. Color: shell—gray to brown, periostracum—yellowish. Size: to 5" (127mm).

Habitat: Found on mud and sand, intertidally to 1,200' (364m).

Range: Gulf of St. Lawrence to North Carolina.

Comments: The Northern Moon Snail is very common. The powerful foot enables this gastropod to plow underneath the sand in search of other mollusks. Upon finding one, it "drills" a hole into the shell with its radula, releases digestive enzymes, and sucks out the somewhat predigested contents. It is common to see the Moon Snail's foot completely enveloping a clam as it feeds on its hapless prey.

SAND COLLAR

The Moon Snail forms the sand collar by embedding its eggs in the sand mass and using mucus to mold this egg ribbon around its shell. The sand collar is flexible in the water but is brittle when found dried on the beach. The eggs are preyed upon by Green Sea Urchins and some gastropods.

Northern Moon Snail mating

(Left) Northern Moon Snail feeding on Razor Clam

(Bottom right) The Sand Collar is the egg mass of the Northern Moon Snail

DATE

LOCATION

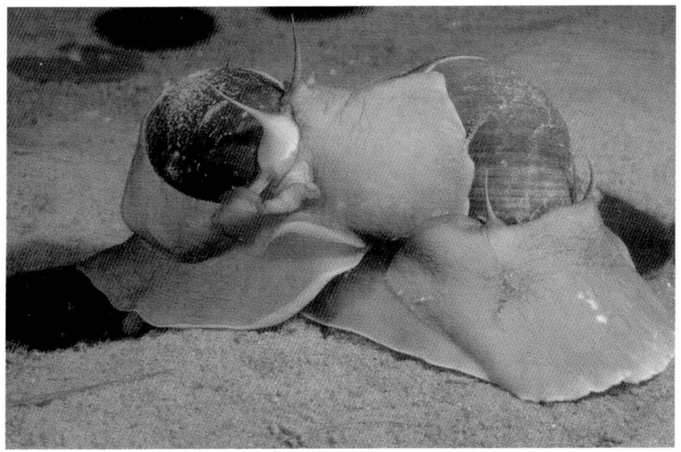

DATE

LOCATION

DATE

LOCATION

LOBED MOON SNAIL *Polinices duplicata*

Identification: This moon snail differs from the Northern Moon Snail, *Lunatia heros,* because its spire is lower and more compressed, appearing to be flatter. Another characteristic feature is the dark, thick callus (absent in *L. heros*) that partially or completely covers the opening of the umbilicus. The operculum is horny. Color: shell—gray to light brown with bluish tinge, mantle—dull gray, two tentacles—yellow with black stripe. Size: to 3" (75mm).

Habitat: Found on sandy and muddy bottoms, intertidally to shallow water.

Range: Massachusetts to Gulf of Mexico.

Comments: Also known as Sharkeye, *P. duplicata* is generally smaller than the Northern Moon Snail.

OYSTER DRILL *Urosalpinx cinerea*

Identification: This very common snail is solid, coarse, and oval shaped, with an elevated spire that is half the length of the shell. There are five to six convex whorls, with about twelve low and rounded wave-like ribs. These are crossed with narrow ridges. The aperture is oval with a short, open anterior canal and sharp outer lip. Color: tan to yellowish or white. Size: to 1" (43mm).

Habitat: Found on rocks, intertidally to 50' (15m).

Range: Nova Scotia to northern Florida.

Comments: The Oyster Drill and sea stars are the two biggest enemies of oyster beds. With its radula, this gastropod drills a small hole into the bivalve's shell, inserts its proboscis, and feeds. The Oyster Drill can not tolerate water with low salinity, but oysters can, so oyster beds are often moved to river mouths. The female Oyster Drill spawns all summer, laying up to twenty-four vase-shaped capsules every two weeks. The eggs adhere to rocks or other hard substrate.

Similar species: The Thick-Lipped Oyster Drill, *Eupleura caudata,* has a thicker outer lip, with large radulae and a longer anterior canal.

ATLANTIC DOGWINKLE *Nucella lapillus*

Identification: The shell is rough, thick, solid, and pointed at both ends. It has five whorls, a short spire, and a blunt apex. The aperture is oval. Color: variable from white to yellow to brown. Size: length, 1½" (38mm); width, 5/8" (15mm).

Habitat: Found on rocks, intertidally.

Range: Labrador to Rhode Island.

Comments: *N. lapillus* is found in large numbers in crevices. Because its food source partially determines the color of the Dogwinkle's shell, those that feed on mussels are brownish, while those that feed on barnacles are shades of white. Rare individuals exhibiting dark brown spiral bands are considered to be the same species. Also known as *Thais lapillus.*

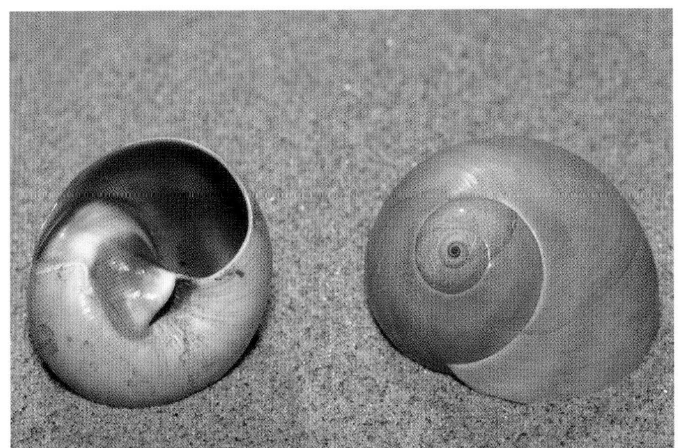

DATE

LOCATION

DATE

LOCATION

DATE

LOCATION

NEW ENGLAND DOG WHELK *Nassarius trivittatus*

Identification: The shell of this common whelk is elongate and ovate with a high, conical spire and a convex body whorl. There are six to seven finely-beaded whorls that are flattened at the shoulder. The aperture is ovate and notched at both ends; the outer lip is thin, and the inner lip is strongly arched. Color: whitish to tan. Size: 3/4" (19mm).

Habitat: Found on sandy or muddy bottoms, intertidally to 300' (91m).

Range: Gulf of St. Lawrence to Florida.

Comments: Also known as the New England Basket Whelk, it is a scavenger and is often found on dead fish and other animals.

EASTERN MUD WHELK *Ilyanassa obsoleta*

Identification: This thick-shelled ovate whelk has a spire half as long as its shell. The apex is blunt and often eroded. The whorls are convex and have distinct suture. Low, flat spiral cords cross the slanting axial ribs. The aperture is oval and purple. Color: reddish brown, but this usually can't be seen due to the coating of mud. Size: length, 1" (25mm); width, 3/8" (9mm).

Habitat: Mudflats, usually near the low-tide line.

Range: Gulf of St. Lawrence to Florida.

Comments: This is the most common snail found on the mudflats. It is omnivorous and, being a scavenger, is often found on dead animals. Also called Common Mud Snail, Mud Dog Whelk.

Eastern Mud Whelk as it is commonly seen, covered with growth

DATE
LOCATION
DATE
LOCATION
DATE
LOCATION

WAVED WHELK *Buccinum undatum*

Identification: This northern whelk's shell has a sharp apex with nine to eighteen waves, or ripples, called axial ribs on each whorl. The shell has five to eight small but distinct spiral chords between each shell section or suture. The periostracum is thick and gives the animal a dirty, gray appearance. The outer lip is wide and leads to a short siphonal canal. The aperture is shining white. Color: chalky-gray Size: to 2½" (62mm).

Habitat: Found subtidally to 600' (180m).

Range: Arctic to New Jersey.

Comments: As a scavenger, this whelk will feed on lobster bait or any dead matter it can find. *B. striatum* is considered the same animal.

Waved Whelk egg mass

TEN-RIDGED WHELK *Neptunea lyrata decemcostata*

Identification: The shell is large, sturdy, and has six to seven whorls. The characteristic feature is a large body whorl with ten winding ridges. The top three ridges continue on to the apex. Color: cream with reddish-brown ridges. Size up to 5" (127mm).

Habitat: Found among rocks, subtidally to 250' (76m).

Range: Nova Scotia to Cape Cod.

Comments: Lobstermen often find these beautiful, carnivorous whelks in their traps. Also known as New England Neptune.

DATE

LOCATION

DATE

LOCATION

DATE

LOCATION

CHANNELED WHELK *Busycon canaliculatum*

Identification: This large, pear-shaped whelk has five to six whorls. It is easily recognized by the deep, channel-like groove along the suture. The body whorl is very large, comprising two-thirds of its height. Color: shell—yellowish gray with a yellow interior; periostracum—brownish with hairs. Size: height, 8" (20cm); width, 5" (127mm).

Habitat: Shallow water on sandy bottoms.

Range: Cape Cod to northern Florida.

Comments: The Channeled Whelk is one of the largest snails on this coast. It is a carnivore and feeds mainly on other mollusks. Eggs are laid in long strings of capsules. When they hatch, baby whelks eat through the casing and emerge as tiny, perfectly formed whelks. The discarded strings of egg capsules are commonly found on the beach. These edible whelks are also called conchs. Native Americans used both whelk and quahog shells for wampum (the equivalent of money).

KNOBBED WHELK *Busycon carica*

Identification: This large, pear-shaped snail has six whorls. The body whorl is large. The thick shell's spire is low, with knobs on the shoulders. The operculum is horny and lacks a periostracum. Color: shell—gray (may have violet streaks when young); aperture—yellow to orange, oval and long. Size: height, 9" (23cm); width, 5" (127mm).

Habitat: Shallow water on sandy bottoms.

Range: Cape Cod to Florida.

Comments: This is the largest snail north of Cape Hatteras. The egg case, often found on beaches, is similar to that of the Channeled Whelk except that the capsules are doubled edged rather than single edged.

(Left) The young Knobbed Whelks leave the egg case when they are miniature, perfectly formed gastropods

(Bottom, right) The egg case of the Knobbed Whelk as it is often found on the beach

DATE

LOCATION

DATE

LOCATION

DATE

LOCATION

STIMPSON'S COLUS *Colus stimpsoni*

Identification: This spindle-shaped whelk is elongate with an extended spire. It has seven to eight low whorls with indistinct sutures. The aperture is oval, the operculum is horny. Color: cream to white with a thin, brownish, velvety periostracum. Size: height, 5" (127mm).

Habitat: On sand and mud bottoms from 5' to 2,500' (1.5m to 760m).

Range: Labrador to Cape Hatteras.

Similar species: Pygmy Whelk, *C. pygmaea,* is smaller and its periostracum is lighter in color.

NAKED SEA BUTTERFLY *Clione limacina*

Identification: The body of this shell-less gastropod is slug-like but has a pointed posterior and a pair of wings at the front. The head has two pairs of tentacles and is separated from the body by a neck-like section. The eyes are located on the posterior pair of tentacles. Color: anterior—pale gray, posterior—red. Size: 1½" (37mm).

Habitat: Coastal and offshore, near the surface.

Range: Arctic to Delaware.

Comments: The Naked Sea Butterfly has a coiled shell in the embryo stage. At some times of the year, these gastropods gather in numbers so large that they color the water. When their population increases to this extent, they become a food source for some whales.

Naked Sea Butterflies mating

DATE

LOCATION

DATE

LOCATION

DATE

LOCATION

WHITE ATLANTIC CADLINA *Cadlina laevis*

Identification: The body is broadly oval, with a ring of feathery gills (generally yellow at the tips) on the dorsal side, at the posterior end. The rhinophores are coil-like. Color: semi-transparent to whitish with yellow spots. Size: length, 1" (25mm); width, 3/8" (9mm).

Habitat: Found on rocky bottoms, subtidally to shallow water.

Range: Arctic to Massachusetts.

Comments: Feeds on sponges.

ROUGH-MANTLED NUDIBRANCH *Onchidoris bilamellata*

Identification: This rough-bodied nudibranch is covered with tubercles. It has a pair of rhinophores near the head and a posterior gill ring; both of which are retractable. Color: reddish brown, cream colored, or tan. Size: 1" (25mm).

Habitat: Found on rocky shores, in crevices, and on encrusting bryozoans, intertidally to subtidally.

Range: Arctic to Rhode Island.

Comments: In the summer, the Rough-Mantled Nudibranch can be found in groups of twenty or thirty as they gather to mate. At this time, they produce a large number of wavy egg masses.

Two Rough Mantled Nudibranchs mating, with an egg mass in the background

DATE

LOCATION

DATE

LOCATION

DATE

LOCATION

WHITE DORID *Onchidoris muricata*

Identification: The body is broadly oval with nearly parallel sides; posterior and anterior are equally rounded. The surface is covered with tubercles that are short, oval, and more abundant toward the margins. There is a pair of retractable rhinophores at the head and one retractable gill ring at the rear. Color: cream-colored to white. Size: length, 1/2"(12mm); width, 1/4" (6mm).

Habitat: Found on and under rocks, intertidally to 25' (7.5m).

Range: Bay of Fundy to Rhode Island.

Comments: The White Dorid is present in all seasons. It feeds on bryozoans.

Eggs of Hairy Doris

HAIRY DORIS *Acanthodoris pilosa*

Identification: The body is broadly oval and is covered with slender, soft, conical tubercles of nearly uniform size. There is one pair of rhinophores, which are equal in size and bent backward. There are seven to nine feather-like gills on the back, at the posterior. Color: white, tan, dark brown, or light yellow. Size: length, 1¼" (32mm); width, 3/8" (10mm).

Habitat: Found under rocks and on algae, from the low-tide line to shallow water.

Range: Arctic to Connecticut.

Comments: Feeds on bryozoans.

DATE

LOCATION

DATE

LOCATION

DATE

LOCATION

RIM-BACKED NUDIBRANCH *Polycera dubia*

Identification: On each side of the body are lateral ridges with projecting cerata-like appendages. Atop the back are small and numerous appendages, with a circle of gills on the middle. Color: body—transparent to whitish, tips of appendages—yellowish. Size: 3/4" (19mm).

Habitat: Found under rocks or on seaweeds, from the low-tide line to shallow water, usually in the vicinity of bryozoans. Intertidally to subtidally.

Range: Arctic to Massachusetts.

Similar Species: *Ancula gibbosa* lacks the lateral ridges of the Rim-Backed Nudibranch.

ROBUST FROND EOLIS *Dendronotus robustus*

Identification: This stout nudibranch is less laterally compressed and less tapered than *D. frondosus.* The skin of the upper side either is smooth or has small tubercles. The anus is located farther toward the anterior end than in other species. There are six or seven pairs of short, thick, branching cerata. The rhinophore is thick and round. Color: reddish body with white spots or gray with yellow dots. Size: to 3" (75mm).

Habitat: Unknown. From shore to 650' (200m). The author has seen this nudibranch only twice, and each time it was on the sand in August at Cape Ann.

Range: Greenland to Cape Cod.

Robust Frond Eolis laying its eggs on a sand collar (the egg mass of another gastropod, the Moon Snail)

DATE

LOCATION

DATE

LOCATION

DATE

LOCATION

ATLANTIC ANCULA *Ancula gibbosa*

Identification: This small nudibranch is thick and elongate, tapering toward the posterior. It has a gill ring on the middle of the back and several cerata-like projections on both sides. Color: body—transparent to whitish, tips of projections—yellowish. Size: 1/2" (12.5mm).

Habitat: Found on seaweeds and rocks, from the low-tide line to shallow water.

Range: Arctic to Massachusetts.

Comments: The Rim-Backed Nudibranch, *Polycera dubia,* is similar but has lateral ridges that are missing in *A. gibbosa.*

BUSHY-BACKED NUDIBRANCH *Dendronotus frondosus*

Identification: This very common nudibranch has a double row of branched cerata along the back. The rhinophores are as long as the first pair of cerata and are quite bushy. Color: body—grayish white with blotches of brown, yellow, or rust; sometimes pure white. Size: to 2" (60mm).

Habitat: Lower intertidal zone to subtidally. Frequents rocky tide pools and places where there are hydroids or fine algal species.

Range: Arctic to Rhode Island.

Comments: Also known as Frond Eolis. The Bushy-Backed Nudibranchs of the north exhibit greater color variations (due to fewer predators) than those of the south.

(Left) A color variant of the Bushy-Backed Nudibranch

Bushy-Backed Nudibranch feeding on hydroids (bottom, right)

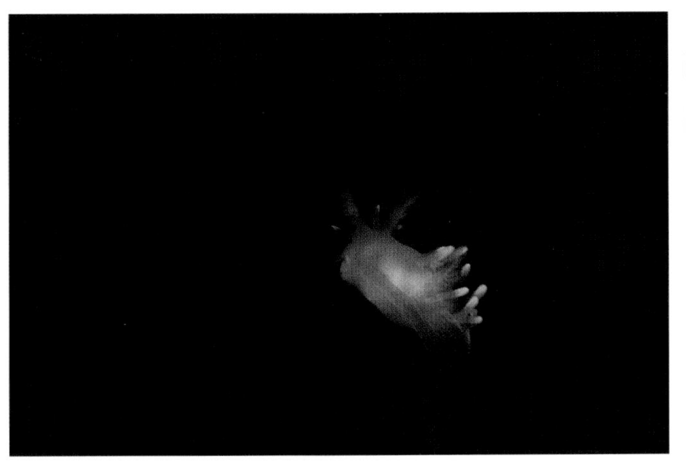

DATE

LOCATION

DATE

LOCATION

DATE

LOCATION

DWARF BALLOON EOLIS *Eubranchus pallidus*

Identification: This small and beautiful nudibranch is uncommon. On each side there are five to ten plump, banded cerata. Color: body—translucent to brownish, cerata—reddish bands. Size: 5/16" (8mm).

Habitat: Found among hydroids, in shallow water.

Range: Arctic to Massachusetts.

Comments: Also known as the Club-Gilled Nudibranch, this animal has been called *Eubranchus exiguus.*

RED-GILLED NUDIBRANCH *Flabellina pellucida*

Identification: It is a characteristic of this genus to have many branchiae (gills), either clustered or elongated, with cores of various shades of red or brown. Each branchia is tipped with opaque white or an opaque white ring. Color: body—opaque white, translucent, or yellowish-white; cerata—various shades of red. Size: to 1 3/16" (30mm).

Habitat: Found on seaweeds and rocks, and around hydroids; from low-tide line to deeper water.

Range: Arctic to Cape Cod.

Comments: *Flabellina verrucosa* is characteristic of this genus. It has orange red cerata with a white ring (rather than one tipped with white) and an opaque white body. *Flabellina pellucida* is a less common northern nudibranch that has a translucent body with clear red cerata that are tipped with white. *Flabellina salmonacea* has a yellowish white body and intense salmon-colored cerata.

Red-gilled Nudibranch, *F. verrucosa*
laying its characteristic spiral egg mass

DATE

LOCATION

DATE

LOCATION

DATE

LOCATION

Red-gilled Nudibranch,
F. pellucida

Two Red-gilled Nudibranchs
feeding on the tentacles of a hydroid

The anterior of a Red-gilled Nudibranch

DATE

LOCATION

DATE

LOCATION

DATE

LOCATION

SALMON-GILLED NUDIBRANCH *Flabellina salmonacea*

Identification: This nudibranch is long and narrow with the posterior tapering to an acute point. The head is large with a V-shaped mouth. The rhinophores are long, and there are about a hundred long cerata. Color: body—translucent to whitish, cerata—salmon-colored. Size: length, 1¾" (44mm); width, 3/8" (9mm).

Habitat: Found in and around algae and rocks, from low tide to deeper water.

Range: Greenland to Massachusetts Bay.

Comments: The Salmon-Gilled Nudibranch feeds on hydroids. In the southern part of its range, it is more common in March and April; in the northern part of its range, it is more common from July to September.

Red-gilled Nudibranch,
F. verrucosa,* variation *chocolata

Red-gilled Nudibranch
***F. verrucosa,* variation *chocolata,* laying egg**

DATE

LOCATION

DATE

LOCATION

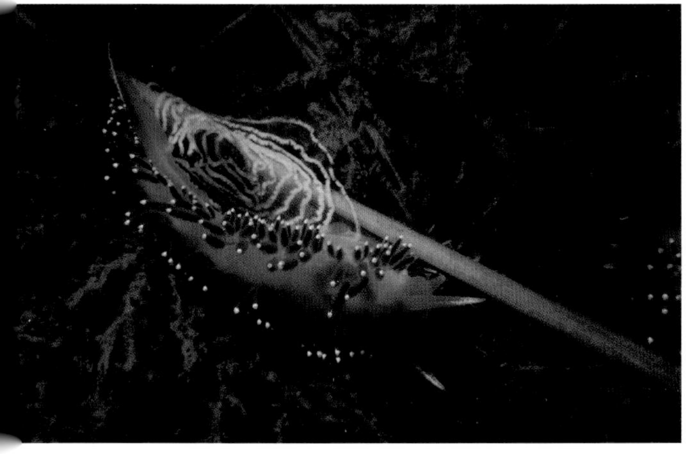

DATE

LOCATION

MANED NUDIBRANCH *Aeolidia papillosa*

Identification: This common nudibranch has many transverse, flattened cerata (up to four hundred per side) in tight rows. Color: variable—spotted with light purple, gray or brown on a brown, gray, or yellowish background. Size: 4" (100mm).

Habitat: Found in tide pools and depths to 600' (200m).

Range: Arctic to Maryland.

Comments: *A. farinacea* is the same animal. Feeds on anemones.

Egg mass of the Maned Nudibranch

Maned Nudibranch feeding on a Frilled Anemone, which is releasing acontia, a powerfu[l] stinging fiber that it uses when greatly stresse[d]

DATE

LOCATION

DATE

LOCATION

DATE

LOCATION

Mollusks/Bivalves

BLUE MUSSEL *Mytilus edulis*

Identification: This smooth filter-feeding bivalve is elongated and narrow ended. It has four to six small, whitish teeth below the beak. It is found attached to rocks, other mussels, or the substrate by byssus threads, which are made of an insoluble protein material secreted by a gland found on the foot. Color: blue black to purple blue. Size: to 4" (100mm).

Habitat: Found on solid substrate, rocky shores, and wharf pilings, intertidally to several feet.

Range: Arctic to South Carolina.

Comments: It was believed that when the Blue Mussel was set in one place, it would anchor itself permanently. We now know that this animal can switch locations by moving its foot, attaching a new byssus thread, and releasing the old one. A single animal can move several feet over several days. Highly edible.

RIBBED MUSSEL *Geukensia demissa*

Identification: The striking feature of this mussel is the radiating ribs on the outside of its shell. Color: variable—mustard to brownish black. Size: 4" (102mm).

Habitat: Found in salt marshes and intertidally in brackish water.

Range: Gulf of St. Lawrence to Florida.

Comments: At one time this species was thought to be inedible, but the author and his friends have eaten ribbed mussels and enjoyed them.

NORTHERN HORSE MUSSEL *Modiolus modiolus*

Identification: A robust, large mussel with a brown black periostracum covered with hairs. This animal's shell has unequal (subterminal) beaks, and the hinge lacks teeth. Color: bluish black, with a white or chalky area near the beaks and tan to brown coloration where the periostracum is shaggy. Size: 6" (150mm).

Habitat: Subtidally to 240' (72m).

Range: Arctic to New Jersey.

Comments: Inedible.

DATE

LOCATION

DATE

LOCATION

DATE

LOCATION

LITTLE BLACK MUSSEL *Musculus niger*

Identification: The shell is oval and thin, and its beaks are close to the front end. The center of the valves is smooth, while the remainder of the surface is covered with thin, concentric growth lines that are crossed by many fine, radiating ribs. Color: interior—shiny silver, exterior—brown to blackish brown (the older mussels are blacker). Size: to 2" (50mm).

Habitat: Found in muddy gravel, from 6' to 360' (2m to 109m).

Range: Greenland to North Carolina.

Comments: Also known as Black Musculus or Black Mussel. Since this is a burrowing mussel, it prefers a soft bottom, which it can move across by using its foot.

ICELAND SCALLOP *Chlamys islandicus*

Identification: The shell is oval; the upper valve is more convex than the lower, but they are equal in size. There are more than fifty thin, radiating ribs with small, erect scales. Some of the ribs are concentrated, forming ridges. The wings on both sides of the umbo are unequal. Color: light orange, reddish brown, purple, yellow, and pink. The lower valve has a paler tone. Some individuals display concentric light and dark bars. Size: length, 4" (102mm).

Habitat: Found on gravel and sand bottoms, 6' to 1,000' (2m to 303m).

Range: Greenland to Cape Cod.

Comments: The upper valve, as in most scallops, is encrusted with tube worms, coralline algae, and other organisms.

DEEP SEA SCALLOP *Placopecten magellanicus*

Identification: Relatively flat and minimally convex as compared with the Bay Scallop. The exterior of the shell has fine, raised, thread-like ridges that give the shell a sandpaper feeling. Color: creamy gray to pinkish purple with lighter rays. Size: to 8"(200 mm).

Habitat: Subtidally in the northern part of its range; to 600' (200m) in the southern part.

Range: Gulf of St. Lawrence to Cape Hatteras.

Comments: This is the common edible sea scallop harvested commercially off our coast. In Maine, divers can find this scallop in shallow water, whereas, it usually appears only in deeper water farther south.

DATE

LOCATION

DATE

LOCATION

DATE

LOCATION

BAY SCALLOP *Aequipecten irradians*

Identification: The shell is almost round with seventeen to eighteen coarse radiating ribs. The wings are large and of equal size. Color: variable—many tones of brown and, at times, even purple near the hinge; the thirty to forty bright blue eyes on the mantle are easily seen when the scallop's valves are apart. Size: 3" (76mm).

Habitat: In shallow water on sandy or muddy bottoms, especially in eel grass.

Range: Generally, from Cape Cod to Texas; has also been reported as far north as Nova Scotia.

Comments: This New England delicacy is able to move quite rapidly by contracting its adductor muscle. The Blue-eyed Scallop, as it is also known, is able to "see" movement because each "eye" has an optic nerve. If you turn the animal over so that the clean valve is on top, the scallop flips itself back to show you which is right-side up.

The "blue eyes" of the Bay Scallop

COMMON OYSTER *Crassostrea virginica*

Identification: The shape is extremely variable; it is affected by the medium on which the oyster grows and by the surrounding location. This massive, unequal, and rough shell is narrow at the hinge but widens gradually. The shell has a mild curve. Size: to 10" (254mm).

Habitat: Water of reduced salinity, intertidally to subtidally, in depths to 40' (12m).

Range: Gulf of St. Lawrence to Gulf of Mexico.

Comments: This is the common edible oyster that is widely consumed throughout the country. The free-swimming larvae go through several stages before they settle down on a solid substrate and become young oysters. At this time they are called "spat." Because the number of oysters depends in part on the quantity of hard substrate, people who "fish" oysters often dump shells, called cultch, over suitable bottom in order to create a new hard surface for future stock. Large oysters can release up to 100 million eggs per spawn, and they may spawn several times in a year. Several species of gastropods and sea stars prey upon this bivalve, and it is subject to several diseases that have devastated Mid-Atlantic stocks in recent years.

DATE

LOCATION

DATE

LOCATION

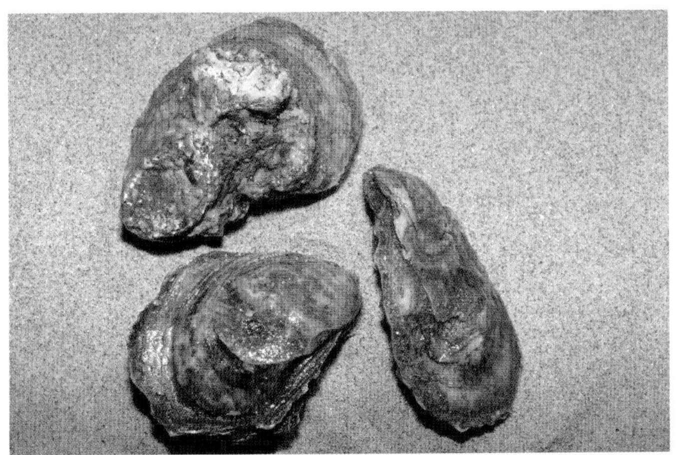

DATE

LOCATION

COMMON JINGLE SHELL *Anomia simplex*

Identification: The shape is circular and irregular. Its form is determined by the object to which it adheres. Color: variable—shades of yellow, white, orange, gray, and even black; has a glossy surface. Size: to 3" (75mm).

Habitat: Attaches to hard substrate such as logs, wharfs, and boats; subtidally to 30' (9m).

Range: Nova Scotia to Texas.

Comments: This is one of the most common shells found on beaches. At certain times during strong storms, large tidal "windrows" of Jingle Shells and Slipper Shells (*Crepidula*) can be found on the shore. During these periods of abundance, people often string up Jingle Shells to make wind chimes.

BLACK QUAHOG *Arctica islandica*

Identification: The Black Quahog has a shape similar to the Hard-Shell Clam (Quahog). In contrast, the Black Quahog is more circular, thinner, has smaller umbos, and a thicker periostracum. It also lacks the pallial sinus and interior purple color of the Hard-Shell Clam. The exterior is smooth except for the growth lines. Color: periostracum—dark brown to black, interior—white. Size: to 4" (100mm).

Habitat: Found in sand, from 30' to 500' (9m to 151m).

Range: Newfoundland to Cape Cod; to North Carolina in deeper water.

Comments: Also known as the Ocean Quahog, Mahogany Clam, or Black Clam, this bivalve is edible.

QUAHOG *Mercenaria mercenaria*

Identification: The shells of this clam are thick and broadly oval. The beaks point toward the anterior. The outside is a dull gray with concentric growth lines. The interior is white with a purple border. Size: length, 3" to 5" (76mm to 127mm); width, 4¼" (107mm).

Habitat: Found in sand or mud in shallow water.

Range: Gulf of St. Lawrence to Florida.

Comments: This large bivalve is also known as the Hard-shelled Clam. It has three different names that correspond to three sizes: Littlenecks are the smallest; Cherrystones are middle sized; and Quahogs are the largest. Littlenecks and Cherrystones are delicious served raw on the half-shell, whereas Quahogs are tougher and are used for chowder. The name Mercenaria is derived from the fact that Native Americans used pieces of the purple-edged shell for wampum.

Similar species: This clam can be confused with *M. campechienis,* the Southern Quahog.

DATE

LOCATION

DATE

LOCATION

DATE

LOCATION

SURF CLAM *Spisula solidissima*

Identification: The shells are large, heavy, and somewhat triangular. The beaks are large and central, with a strong hinge. The surface of the valves is smooth, with fine concentric lines. Color: shell—yellowish white, periostracum—olive to brown. Size: length, 8" (20cm); height, 5½" (14cm).

Habitat: Found in sand and mud, from the low-tide line to 100' (30m).

Range: Nova Scotia to South Carolina.

Comments: The Surf Clam, now an important commercial shellfish, is used principally for canning and as fish bait. Hungry gulls are often seen carrying and dropping these clams onto hard surfaces in order to break the shell.

A Surf Clam uses its foot to pull itself under the sand. (The previous photo shows the Surf Clam extending its foot into the sand.)

(Bottom left) The siphons of the Surf Clam

(Bottom right) A Surf Clam releasing sperm into the water

DATE

LOCATION

DATE

LOCATION

COMMON RAZOR CLAM *Ensis directus*

Identification: This common, long, narrow clam looks very similar to a barber's straight-edged razor. It is slightly to moderately curved, it shows concentric growth lines, and the edges are quite sharp. Each shell has a long posterior tooth and two vertical cardinal teeth. Color: brownish green. Size: to 10" (25cm), about six times longer than it is wide.

Habitat: Found on sand flats, from the low-tide line to shallow water.

Range: Labrador to Florida.

Comments: Edible. Has the ability to dig itself quickly into the sand. Preyed upon by the Northern Moon Snail.

The siphons of the Razor Clam

SOFT-SHELL CLAM *Mya arenaria*

Identification: This clam is known regionally as a "steamer" In live individuals, there is a very noticeable gap between the valves at the posterior end. Color: periostracum—light gray to whitish gray. Size: to 4" (100mm).

Habitat: Found on mudflats or in a mixture of sand and mud, intertidally to subtidally.

Range: Arctic to North Carolina.

Comments: This clam has been harvested by man since prehistoric times and has provided a tremendous amount of protein. Human overpopulation and the resulting pollution of intertidal clam flats have jeopardized this once abundant mollusk and made some stocks unfit for human consumption. Bacterial, viral, and heavy metal contamination have also endangered the species. Also known as Long Clam or Nannynose. Preyed upon by seabirds, raccoons, and green crabs.

DATE

LOCATION

DATE

LOCATION

DATE

LOCATION

TRUNCATE SOFT-SHELL CLAM *Mya truncata*

Identification: The valves are oblong (almost rectangular) and thin, with moderate beaks. The anterior end is rounded, while the posterior is truncated, with a wide, flaring gap. The surface is wrinkled. Color: dull white with yellowish brown periostracum. Size: to 3" (75mm).

Habitat: Found in sand and mud, intertidally to 100' (30m).

Range: Arctic to Massachusetts.

Comments: In the Soft-Shell Clam, *M. arenaria,* the pallial sinus is tongue-shaped, but in *M. truncata,* the pallial sinus flares.

GREAT PIDDOCK *Zirfaea crispata*

Identification: In the sturdy valves of the Great Piddock, a groove runs from the umbo to the margin of the shell and divides each valve into almost equal parts. The anterior region has radiating, fold-like wrinkles that form a serrated edge; the posterior region has irregular growth lines. Both ends of the valves gap widely; the posterior end is evenly rounded, while the anterior is pointed. Color: gray to white. Size: to 3" (76mm).

Habitat: Found in soft substrate such as peat, mud, or clay; intertidally to shallow depths.

Range: Labrador to New Jersey.

Comments: The siphons of the Great Piddock can be found extending 2" above the sand and look like tunicates. The Great Piddock is capable of boring into wood as well as the above-mentioned soft substrate.

The siphons of the Great Piddock

DATE

LOCATION

DATE

LOCATION

DATE

LOCATION

LONG-FINNED SQUID *Loligo pealei*

Identification: The anterior portion of the mantle (body) is circular and tapers to a point at the posterior. The fins are long, at least half the length of the mantle. The fins meet at the pointed end of the body. The head has large eyes, which are covered by a transparent skin, and there is a pair of tentacles that are longer than the arms. There are four pairs of arms, each measuring half the length of the mantle. Color: changeable—may be white or mottled with brown or purple.

Habitat: Found at all depths, subtidally to 600' (182m).

Range: Maine to Florida.

Comments: This squid is very common in New England from April to November. The egg clusters are communal. They are deposited and attached to algae and other available substrate. Each gelatinous, finger-like capsule is 2" (51mm) long and holds up to two hundred eggs. The embryo can be seen swimming in the capsule before it hatches. This abundant squid is highly prized as food. It is preyed upon by Bluefish, Striped Bass, and other predatory species of fish.

Long-Finned Squid with eggs

(Left) Lobster feeding on the eggs of a Long-Finned Squid

(Bottom right) The eggs are brownish when they are ready to hatch

DATE

LOCATION

DATE

LOCATION

DATE

LOCATION

ANNELIDA
(Polychaetes)

Members of this phylum are segmented worms whose bodies are divided into many similar parts. Representatives of this phylum are found in most types of habitats, including the garden variety earthworm. Annelids have a body plan that is more advanced than the previous levels of phyla. It can be said that Annelids are organized on the "system" level. They have complete nervous, circulatory, digestive and excretory systems. The gut is a straight tube extending from mouth to anus. Respiration takes place through the skin, or cuticle, although some annelids have gills.

The class of worms that is primarily marine is called Polychaeta, which means many bristles. They abound in the oceans, live near the shore, and hide in sand burrows. In Class Polychaeta, there are two sub-classes, Errantia and Sedentaria.

Errant worms move about by using contractions of their muscles and/or by movement of appendages for swimming. They have paired appendages (parapodia) with bristles (setae), similar body segments, and sensory appendages on the head. The parapodia function like oars to propel the animal through the water. The clamworm, *Nereis virens,* is typical of the errant worms. It is often seen by divers and used as bait for fishing. It has two hard, black teeth embedded in the muscle tissue of the pharynx on either side of the mouth. When it captures food, it thrusts out its teeth, extends the pharynx, and turns the mouth inside out. This is called an eversible pharynx and mouth, which is typical of errant worms. When the worm bites into food, it can pull the food deep into its pharynx. The bite from these worms can be painful, as many who fish can attest.

In contrast, sedentary worms do not have sensory appendages but often have many gills or feeding tentacles which may be retracted rapidly into the body tube. The body segments are quite different and often taper to a point at the rear. They are sessile and live their lives in vertical or U-shaped holes in the substrate or in rock crevices. Their bristles (setae) may have hooked tips to help hold them in their burrows. Feather-duster worms are beautiful examples of sedentary polychaetes.

Feeding behavior varies in this class of marine worms. Errant worms move about as predators or bottom-deposit feeders. From the safety of their burrows, sedentary worms are filter feeders or bottom-deposit feeders.

Sexes are separate in most polychaetes. Eggs and sperm are released in the water column where fertilization takes place externally. Copulation is rare in polychaetes.

Sedentary Worm

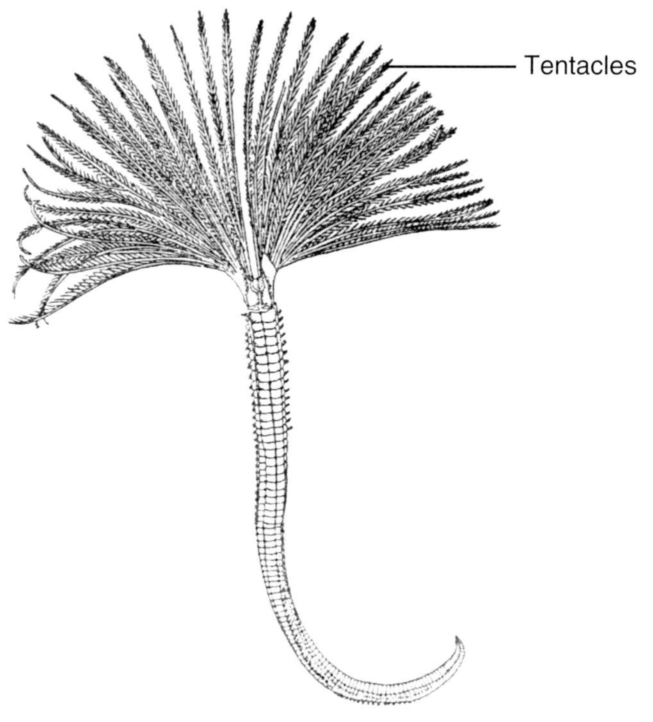

Clam Worm

LEAFY PADDLE WORM *Phyllodoce* sp.

Identification: Like other members of its family, this carnivorous polychaete worm has leafy or paddle-shaped parapodial cirri. The head features four pairs of long tentacles. Above the mouth there is a cone- or heart-shaped lobe that has four short antennae. There are two eyes and no jaws. The dorsal and ventral cirri are leaf shaped. Color: greenish. Size: length, 17" (43cm); width, 3/8" (9mm).

Habitat: Found around holdfasts of algae, on gravel bottoms, and under rocks; from low-tide line to over 4,000' (1219m).

Range: Arctic to Gulf of Mexico.

Comments: Feeds on other worms and small animals.

PLANKTON WORM *Tomopteris helgolandica*

Identification: This wonderful worm is transparent. The parapodia are long and paddle-like. The adult has a distinct cylindrical tail. Size: 3½" (88mm).

Habitat: The entire Atlantic Ocean, from the surface to 6,000' (1830m).

Comments: *T. helgolandica* is found throughout the year. It migrates vertically and is often seen at night.

TWELVE-SCALED WORM *Lepidonotus squamatus*

Identification: This short, wide worm has twelve to thirteen pairs of rough, oval scales that are covered with small, round tubercles. The tentacles and the antennae exhibit dark bands. Color: body—brownish or gray or mottled with both; projections on scales—tan, greenish, or reddish. Size: length, 2" (51mm); width, 5/8" (16mm).

Habitat: Found around and under rocks, on gravel bottoms, from low tide line to 8,000' (2438m).

Range: Labrador to Chesapeake Bay.

Comments: When disturbed, it rolls up into a ball. Unlike some other scaled worms, this one does not readily lose its scales.

DATE

LOCATION

DATE

LOCATION

DATE

LOCATION

FIFTEEN-SCALED WORM *Harmothoe imbricata*

Identification: This short, wide worm has thirty-seven segments and is somewhat flat. It is covered with fifteen pairs of thin, smooth scales. The head narrows to two blunt points; on the underside are four eyes that are not visible from above. Color: variable—reddish, brown, greenish, black, and gray. Size: length, 2½" (64mm); width, 3/4" (18mm).

Habitat: Found around and under rocks, intertidally to as deep as 11,000' (3353m). *H. imbricata* is also able to live in brackish water.

Range: Arctic to New Jersey.

Comments: The Fifteen-Scaled Worm has been known to live in shells used by hermit crabs.

Similar species: Another Fifteen-Scaled Worm that is found in the same area, *H. extenuata,* also has four eyes, but these are visible from above.

CLAM WORM *Nereis virens*

Identification: The head region is thicker than the body, which tapers toward the rear. In a mature adult there are up to 200 segments with well-developed parapodia. The head has four pairs of cirri, four eyes, one pair of palps, and an eversible proboscis with jaws. Color: iridescent green, brown, or blue. Size: generally 6" to 8" (150 to 200mm) long, but individuals measuring 36" (90cm) long and 1¾" (44mm) wide have been reported.

Habitat: Found in sand, mud, or peat bottoms in protected bays and brackish estuaries, from the high-tide line to 600' (175m).

Range: Maine to Virginia.

Comments: This worm is commonly used as bait in fishing. It aggressively feeds on other worms, other invertebrates, and algae. It has a very good sense of smell that enables it to locate food quickly.

The parapodia on each segment of the Clam Worm

DATE

LOCATION

DATE

LOCATION

DATE

LOCATION

EYED-FRINGED WORM *Cirratulus cirratus*

Identification: The body is elongate and cylindrical, with a conical head that has two to nine pairs of black eyes on top. The eyes may be grouped together to form an arc. It does not have palps. There are long filaments on the first bristle-bearing segment. Color: yellow to orange. Size: length, 4¾" (121mm); width, 1/8" (3mm).

Habitat: Found under rocks and sponges, subtidally to shallow water.

Range: Maine to Cape Cod.

Comments: The Eyed-Fringed Worm builds its tubes under rocks and extends its fragile tentacles onto the substratum to gather food.

RED TEREBELLID WORM *Polycirrus eximius*

Identification: On the head of this sedentary worm are many tentacles that characteristically extend in many directions. The body tapers toward the rear and has twenty-five segments. Each has a bundle of bristles, or setae. It lacks gills and eyes. Color: tentacles—red, body—red becoming yellowish toward the posterior. Size: length, 2¾" (70mm); width, 1/4" (6mm).

Habitat: Found in sand or mud, under rocks and in eel grass, from low-tide line to 55' (17m).

Range: Maine to North Carolina.

Comments: The Red Terebellid Worm has no circulatory system, but its body fluid contains many red blood cells. The worm extends its tentacles by forcing red blood cells into them.

JOHNSTON'S ORNATE WORM *Amphitrite johnstoni*

Identification: The body tapers from a thick thorax to a more slender abdomen. The head has many long, yellow tentacles and three pairs of branching, blood-red gills. Of the many segments, there are setae on twenty-four to twenty-five segments. Color: reddish, pinkish, or brownish. Size: length, 10" (25cm); width, 1/2" (12mm).

Habitat: Found on soft bottoms, under rocks and other objects, from low-tide line to shallow water.

Range: Arctic to New Jersey.

Comments: Usually all that one sees of *A. johnstoni* is the head and tentacles since it lives under rocks in a tube composed of mucus mixed with sand or mud. The worm extends its grooved and mucus-covered tentacles to sweep the bottom for food. Small organic particles return to the mouth as if on a conveyor belt. Identification is often difficult because there are twenty species that have the same basic body plan.

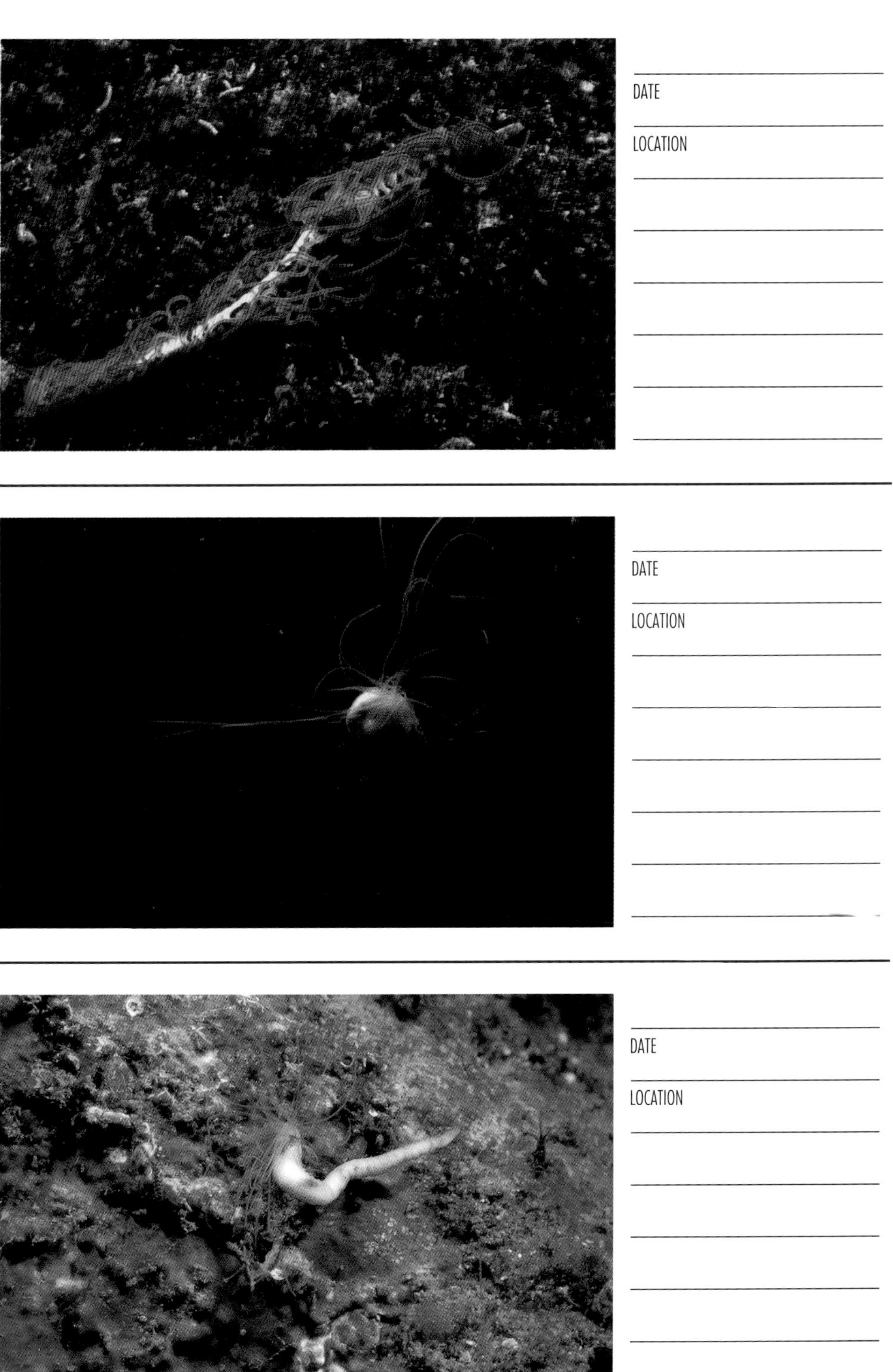

DATE

LOCATION

DATE

LOCATION

DATE

LOCATION

FAN (SABELLID) WORM *Sabella* sp.

Identification: The body is somewhat round, stout, and tapered. There are five to twelve segments, with bristles in the thorax. The head has two plume-like tentacles that originate from either side of the mouth. These form a branchial crown that serves both for feeding and respiration. Color: tube—brownish and tan, tentacles—reddish to brown. Size: to 4" (102mm).

Habitat: Found on pilings, attached to floats, and in rock crevices; intertidally to shallow water.

Range: Maine to Florida.

Comments: Sabellid Worms secrete mucus to build a cylindrical tube to which mud and sand adhere. When disturbed, the tentacles can quickly withdraw into the tube for protection. The animal uses its tentacles to catch small particles of food suspended in the water.

SLIME (FAN) WORM *Myxicola infundibulum*

Identification: This sedentary worm builds a mucus tube that tapers toward the posterior and is buried in the substratum. There is a feather-like whorl of gills that form a membrane. These feather-like tentacles are called radioles. Color: gills, pinkish, yellowish, bluish, or brownish. Size: length, 8" (20 cm); width, 1¼" (31mm).

Habitat: Found in the substrate among rocks, gravel, and other sessile animals, from low tide line to 170' (52m).

Range: Arctic to New York.

Comments: The Fan Worm has a sensitive nerve fiber and can instantly withdraw into its cavity when it senses the presence of another animal. After withdrawing, the only thing that is visible is a slimy mass of mucus. Therefore, this animal is difficult for divers to observe at close range.

(Left) These Slime Worms—above the sea star—have their tentacles, or radioles, extended

(Bottom right) Slime Worms retract their tentacles when disturbed

DATE

LOCATION

DATE

LOCATION

DATE

LOCATION

SINISTRAL SPIRAL TUBE WORM *Spirorbis borealis*

Identification: This small, snail-like tube adheres to seaweeds. As it grows, it coils counterclockwise from the opening to the center of the coil. The head has one modified tentacle (it looks like a one-sided paddle) that serves as an operculum. Color: whitish. Size: 1/8" (3mm).

Habitat: Found intertidally, on the fronds of seaweeds such as Irish Moss, *Chondrus crispus,* and *Fucus* sp.; also attaches itself to any hard surface.

Range: Bay of Fundy to Cape Cod.

Comments: This tiny, calcareous tube worm looks like a snail glued to seaweed. Unlike most polychaete worms, it is hermaphroditic; that is, it has male gonads in the rear section of the abdomen and female gonads in the front section.

Similar species: The Dextral Spiral Tube Worm, *S. spirillum,* which coils clockwise.

LACY TUBE WORM *Filograna implexa*

Identification: These small worms grow in intertwining bundles of thin white tubes. Color: purple to pink. Size: Tubes—length, 2½" (63mm); width, 1/8" (3mm). Worm—length, 1/4" (6mm); width, 1/25" (1mm). Bundle or group—1' (30cm) across.

Habitat: Found on rocks, from below the low-tide line to 170' (51m).

Range: Maine to Cape Cod.

Comments: The Lacy Tube Worm looks like bundles of spaghetti or frayed rope. It can reproduce both sexually and asexually (through binary fission). The animal can divide into two sections and regenerate the missing parts.

DATE

LOCATION

DATE

LOCATION

DATE

LOCATION

ARTHROPODA

There are more than one million known species of Arthropods. All but 85,000 are insects. Every member of this group has jointed legs; in most, the body is segmented and covered by a hard, chitinous exoskeleton. These animals are found in practically all types of habitats.

Horseshoe Crabs and Sea Spiders are in separate classes within Phylum Arthropoda. The Horseshoe Crab has a cephalothorax covered by a U-shaped carapace and five pairs of walking legs. Found in ancient fossil records, its little-changed body plan has survived the test of time. There are only four living species today, one in the Northwest Atlantic and the rest in waters of Eastern Asia. Sea Spiders have eight to twelve walking legs and four simple eyes. Although largely unknown to the average person, they are actually quite common. If you look carefully among the bryozoans on wharf pilings, you will surely find them.

Most marine arthropods are in the class Crustacea, which comprises many subdivisions including barnacles, shrimp, lobsters, and crabs. In higher crustaceans, the body plan includes a head, a thorax, and an abdomen. The head area may have five segments with two pairs of antennae. Mouth parts are composed of two pairs of maxillae and one pair of mandibles. The thorax has eight segments and carries the limbs used for locomotion. The abdomen consists of six segments with swimming feet and a final segment called the telson. Lobsters are good representatives of this body arrangement. In other arthropods, the cephalic (head) area is fused with the thorax into one piece. The covering of this cephalothorax is called the carapace; posterior to the cephalothorax is the abdomen.

A significant advance seen in Arthropods is the exoskeleton. A strong defense, the prevention of water loss, and the provision of an area for muscle attachment are advantages of the exoskeleton. The major disadvantage is that it does not grow as the animal grows. To increase in size, the arthropod must go through a process called molting. First, a new, soft exoskeleton begins forming under the old one. The old exoskeleton then splits, and the animal climbs out. At this time, it is very vulnerable to predation and usually finds a hiding place until the new exoskeleton hardens. Arthropods can molt one or more times yearly.

Another Arthropod advance is their method of locomotion: jointed legs that enable quicker, more flexible mobility. However, not all appendages are used for locomotion. Their functions may be sensory, respiratory, or sexual. Appendages are often specialized, serving a single function that can vary from animal to animal.

Crustaceans have adapted to many habitats and feeding strategies. Many are omnivorous scavengers, some are strictly carnivores, others are herbivores.

Most Arthropods are dioecious (either male or female.) Copulation and internal fertilization are characteristic of most of the species. It is common to see the female crab, shrimp, or lobster with eggs attached to the abdomen.

Shrimp

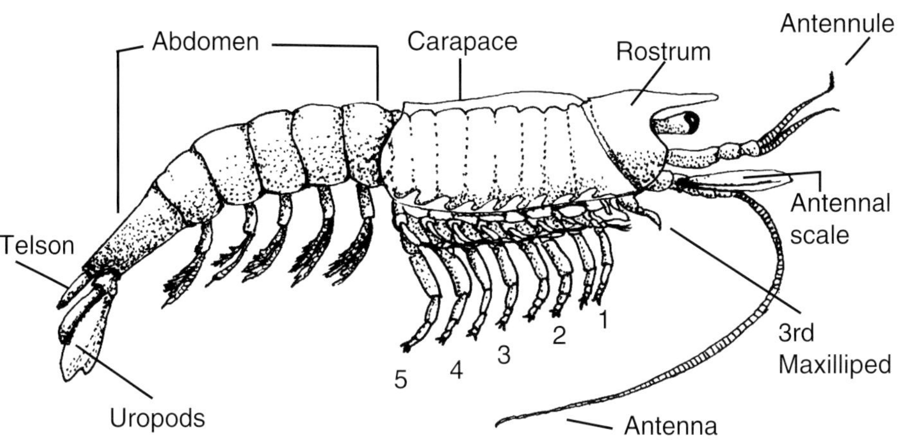
Abdomen
Carapace
Rostrum
Antennule
Antennal
scale
Telson
1
2
3
4
5
3rd
Maxilliped
Uropods
Antenna

Crab

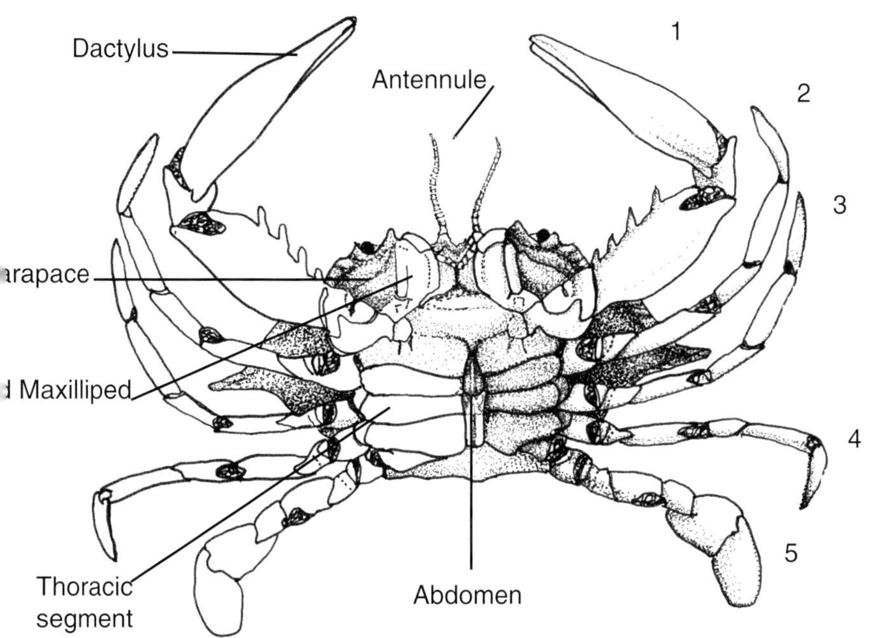
Dactylus
Antennule
1
2
3
arapace
d Maxilliped
4
5
Thoracic
segment
Abdomen

LENTEL SEA SPIDER *Anopodactylus lentus*

Identification: This common pycnogonid has a slender body and four pairs of long legs (males have an extra pair). The proboscis is long and rounded with slender chelifores. The leg-like palpi are lacking. Color: greenish, brownish, or reddish purple. Size: body—length, 1/4" (6mm); legs—length, 3/4" (19mm).

Habitat: Found among hydroids and tunicates, intertidally to deep water.

Range: Bay of Fundy to Florida.

Comments: This species has longer legs than any other sea spider on this coast. It feeds on hydroids.

Similar species: The Clawed Sea Spider, *Phoxichilidium femoratum* (common north of Cape Cod), is similar but has terminal claws with a distinct auxiliary claw. By contrast, that of the Lentel Sea Spider is vestigal.

Lentel Sea Spider mating

ANEMONE SEA SPIDER *Pycnogonum littorale*

Identification: This sea spider has a broad, stubby, flat body with a conical proboscis. There are four small black eyes located behind the proboscis. Chelifores are absent; the abdomen is small and slender. This spider's walking legs are stout, and the male has accessory legs that are used for carrying the eggs. Color: yellow brown to brown. Size: 1/2" (13mm).

Habitat: Found under rocks near sea anemones; near the low-tide line to shallow water.

Range: Gulf of St. Lawrence to Long Island, New York.

Comments: Often found on the sides or base of the Frilled Anemone. It feeds by penetrating the tissue of the anemone with its proboscis. This does not seem to disturb the anemone, since it does not react defensively.

DATE

LOCATION

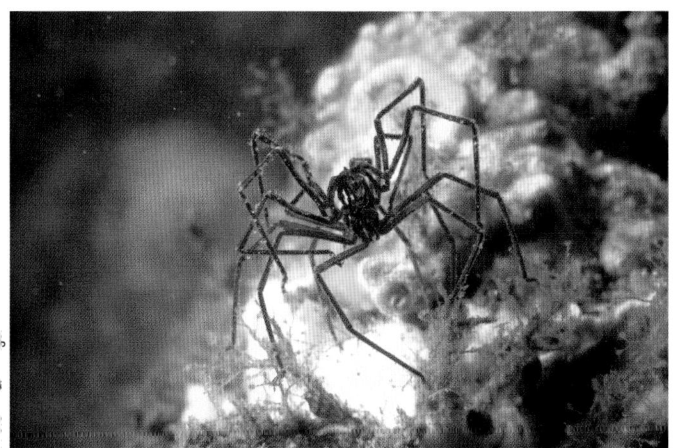

DATE

LOCATION

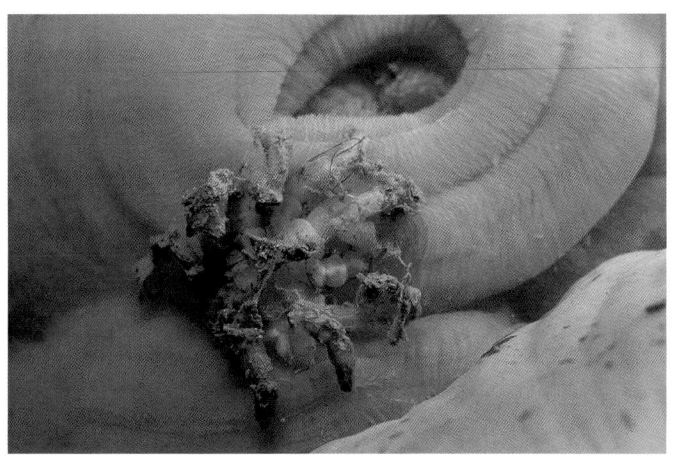

DATE

LOCATION

ATLANTIC HORSESHOE CRAB *Limulus polyphemus*

Identification: The carapace is horseshoe shaped and convex, with a spike-like telson (tail). The crab does not use the telson as a weapon but as a means to right itself if it has been turned over. There are two pairs of compound eyes. Each side of the abdomen has six spines. Underneath, a pair of pinchers is located in front of the mouth. Around the mouth are five pairs of walking legs. On the male, the legs in the first pair are rounded and thick; they are used to hold on to the female during mating season. At the narrow end of the carapace are the book gills, which are used for respiration. Color: greenish brown. Size: length, to 2' (61cm); width, to 12" (30cm).

Habitat: Found on sand or mud bottoms, intertidally to 75' (23m).

Range: Maine to Gulf of Mexico.

Comments: This living fossil (180 million years old) has an interesting history. It is not actually a crab but a distant relative of the spider. At one time it was believed to feed on clams, so there was a bounty on it. Farmers used these crabs as fertilizer. Today, the blue blood of *L. polyphemus* is very valuable in the field of medicine because it can determine the presence of toxins in serums. The way in which the animal reproduces is also interesting. In the spring, the female releases a pheromone into the water. The male uses this to locate her. When he finds her, he holds on to her carapace with his specialized claws. This ensures that he will be there (to fertilize the eggs) when she goes ashore to deposit them in the sand. Mating occurs in May during the high tide and the full moon.

Male Horseshoe Crab holding on to larger female

(Left) Horseshoe Crab using its tail, or telson, to turn itself over

(Bottom right) Three male Horseshoe Crabs fertilizing the eggs that a female is depositing in the sand

DATE

LOCATION

DATE

LOCATION

DATE

LOCATION

NORTHERN ROCK BARNACLE *Semibalanus balanoides*

Identification: This large, conical barnacle has a rough surface and strongly ribbed plates with grooves on the inside. The sides have two pairs of plates that overlap one of two unpaired plates. On top, there are two pairs of plates with a space between. Color: grayish white. Size: height and width, 2" (50mm).

Habitat: Found on rocks, subtidally to 500' (152m).

Range: Arctic to Cape Cod.

Comments: The scientific name means "acorn" in Latin.

ROUGH BARNACLE *Balanus balanus*

Identification: The shape of this common barnacle is variable; it is usually conical, but in dense colonies, it can be twisted and elongated. The shell is usually rough and folded. The plates are porous on the inside. When young, the plates are smooth on the outside, but later they develop four to five vertical grooves and are scalloped at the base. One distinguishing feature of this species is the operculum, which has two valves that are pointed at the tip and two that are blunt, creating deep notch at the top. Color: white. Size: height, 1" (25mm); width, 1/2" (13mm).

Habitat: Found on hard surfaces, intertidally to shallow water.

Range: Arctic to Delaware.

Comments: Feeds on plankton by extending its cirri into the water like small whips.

IVORY BARNACLE *Balanus eburneus*

Identification: The plates are ivory white and smooth. The tergum has a deep indented spur. It is tube-like and flat on top. Size: 1" (25mm).

Habitat: On solid substrate in bays and estuaries; near the low-tide line and below, in shallow water.

Range: Maine to South America.

Comments: Considered by boat owners to be a fouling organism, since it can cover a hull in a short period of time.

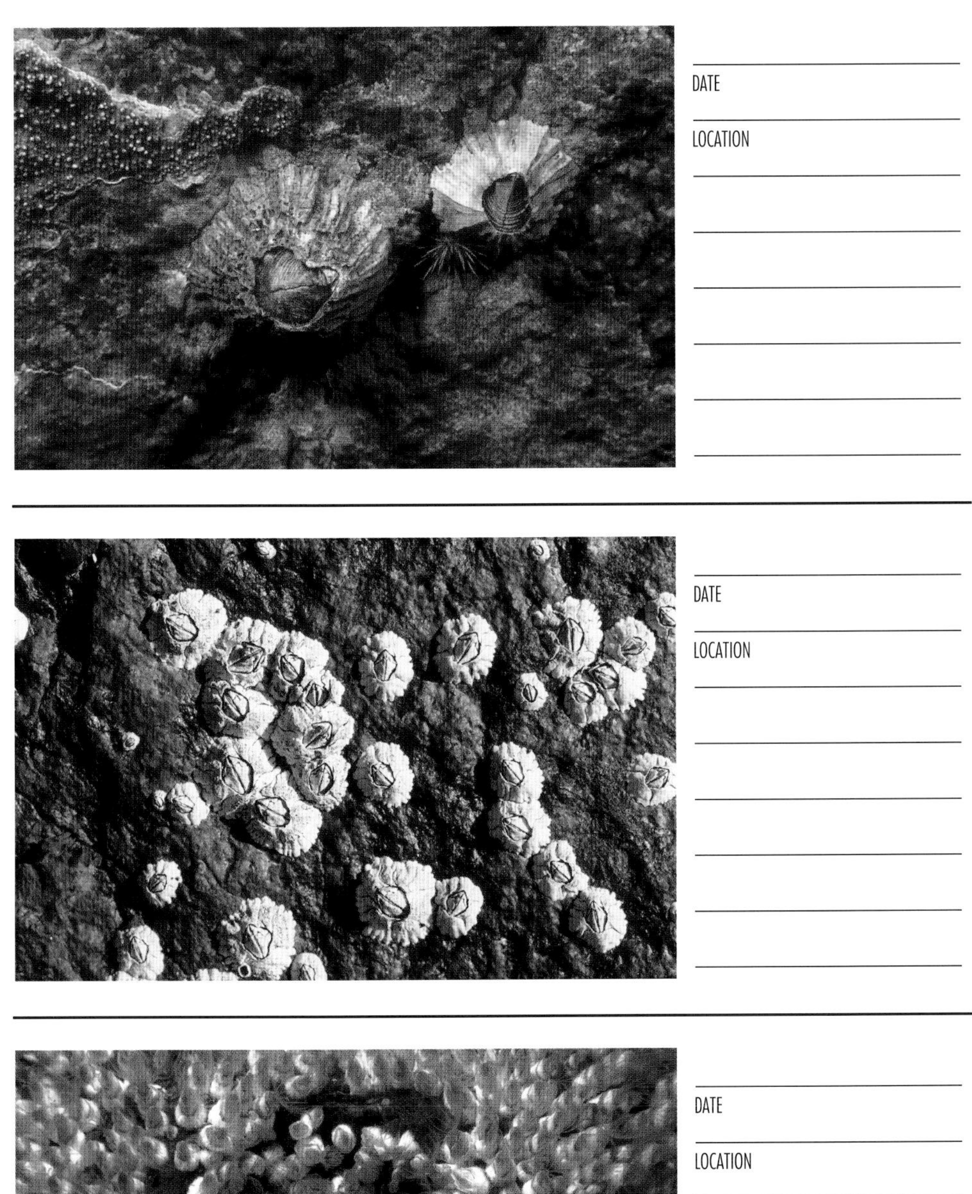

DATE

LOCATION

DATE

LOCATION

DATE

LOCATION

BALTIC ISOPOD *Idotea baltica*

Identification: The body is broad, ovate, and somewhat flat. There are seven thoracic segments, each with a pair of similar legs. The first pair of antennae has a single-jointed flagellum; the second pair is directed frontward and bent laterally. The eyes are large and on the side of the head. Color: variable, often mottled—dark green, reddish, brownish, or tannish in many patterns. Size: length, 1" (25mm); width, 1/4" (6mm).

Habitat: Found in shallow water on the bottom on rocks and algae, or on floating algae.

Range: Gulf of St. Lawrence to North Carolina.

Comments: The Baltic Isopod is very common, and one can see many of these bug-like creatures by examining seaweed.

Baltic Isopod color variation

HEDGEHOG AMPHIPOD *Paramphitoe hystrix*

Identification: This small, flat, oval-shaped amphipod has two pairs of antennae. The second pair is longer than the first. The abdominal surface is covered with tubercles laterally and dorsally. The eyes are red. Color: yellow to tan. Size: 1" (25mm).

Habitat: Found on rocks and sponges (especially vase-shaped sponges) from the low-tide line to 300' (100m).

Range: Arctic to Maine.

Comments: The Hedgehog Amphipod is generally associated with sponges. The water current created by the host sponge draws in nutrients that are beneficial to the amphipod.

DATE

LOCATION

DATE

LOCATION

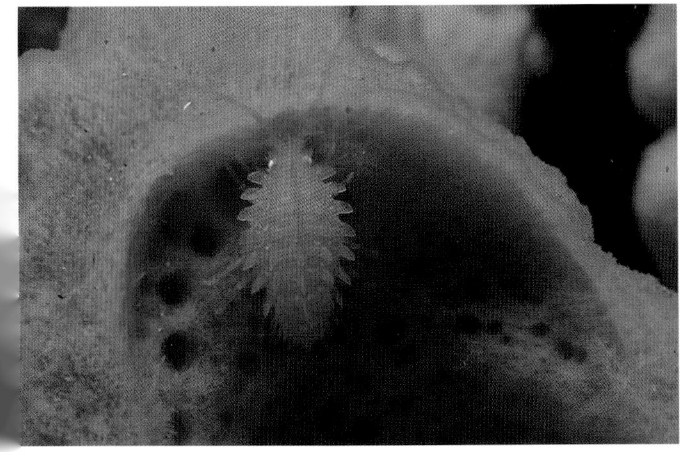

DATE

LOCATION

SKELETON SHRIMP *Caprella* sp.

Identification: The Skeleton Shrimp is a unique amphipod. Its body gives the appearance of a praying mantis and consists of a series of cylindrical joints. The round head and the thoracic segment are somewhat fused. The second segment has the mantis-like claws; the third and fourth have paddle-shaped gills; and the last three have grasping appendages. The stomach is just a small button. There are two pairs of antennae, the first being longer than the second. Color: colorless to reddish or tan. Size: 3/4" (18mm), but some species are 2" (51mm).

Habitat: Found on seaweeds, hydroids, sponges, and other growth from the low-tide line to 7,450' (2271m).

Range: Arctic to North Carolina.

Comments: This slow moving amphipod holds on to the seaweed with its last appendages and stands up like a praying mantis, ready to snare its prey.

Skeleton Shrimp

(Bottom left) Skeleton Shrimp

(Bottom right) Skeleton Shrimp on sea peach

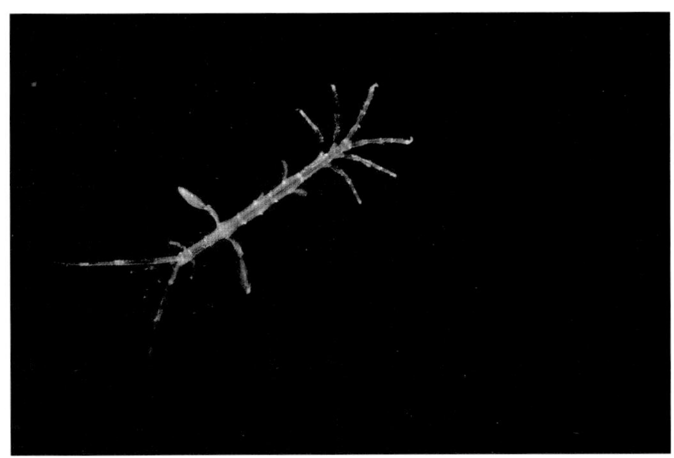

DATE

LOCATION

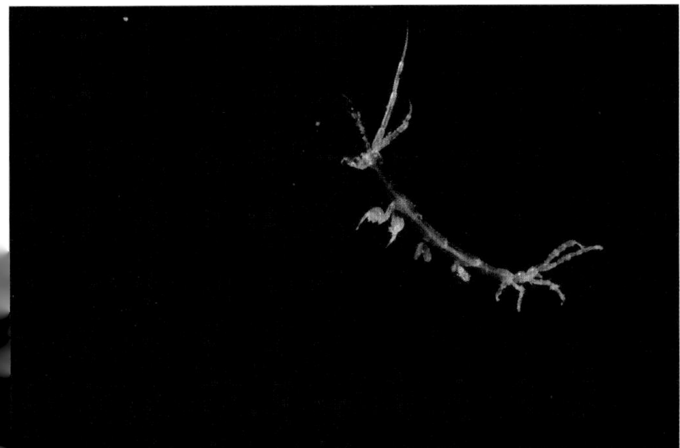

DATE

LOCATION

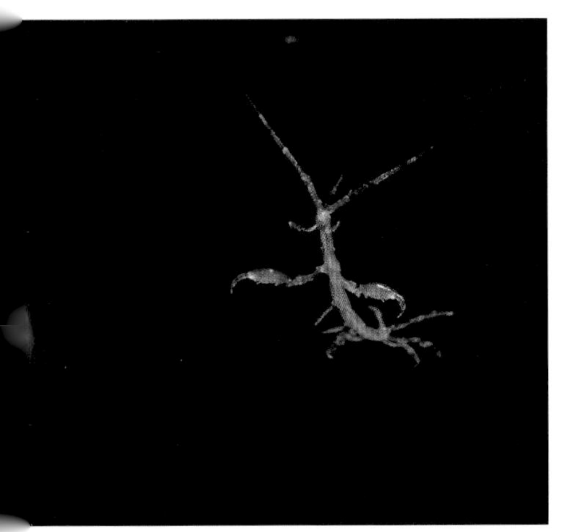

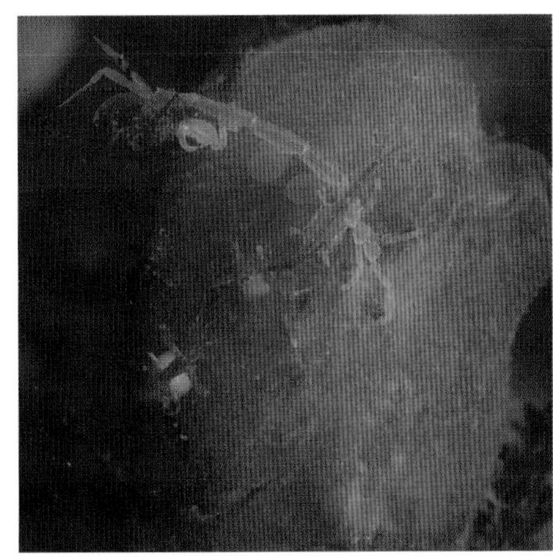

MYSID SHRIMP *Mysis* sp.

Identification: This common group of shrimp is small, translucent, and easily missed. The two anterior appendages nearest the mouth are specialized, while the eight thoracic appendages have two branches each. Color: translucent, greenish, or light yellow, with occasional dark markings. Size: 1/2" (12mm).

Habitat: Subtidal around bays and estuaries. Adults found on bottom; young are free-swimming.

Range: Gulf of St. Lawrence to New Jersey.

Comments: If a hand lens or microscope is available, species identification can be completed by comparing antennae, telson shape, and spines.

The Sand Shrimp's coloration conceals it well

SAND SHRIMP *Crangon septemspinosa*

Identification: This shrimp has a short, dorsally flattened rostrum, with only one spine, or tooth, midway on the carapace. First pair of walking legs is subchelate (claw-like). Color: almost transparent to opaque with a greenish tint, mottled with brown or black. Size: to 3" (76mm).

Habitat: Found on sandy bottoms and eel grass, from tide pools to shallow water.

Range: Arctic to Chesapeake Bay.

Comments: This is a very common small shrimp along our shores. Bluefish, flounders, and striped bass are the principal predators of this shrimp. *Crangon septemspinosus* and *Crangon vulgaris* are synonyms.

DATE

LOCATION

DATE

LOCATION

DATE

LOCATION

MONTAGUE'S SHRIMP *Pandalus montagui*

Identification: This shrimp has a smooth carapace, and the anterior part of the rostrum is toothless but curves up slightly. It lacks a middle spine on the abdomen. The second right walking leg has twenty segments. Color: pink to red, or red stripes in young. Size: to 5" (127mm).

Habitat: Found subtidally to open ocean.

Range: Arctic to Rhode Island.

Comments: Edible. Also known as Northern Boreal Shrimp.

Montague's Shrimp

POLAR SHRIMP *Lebbeus polaris*

Identification: The body is elongated with a short, slender rostrum. There are two teeth on the carapace, three to five teeth on top of the rostrum, and two to four below the rostrum. Color: carapace—reddish-brown to red, and transparent. Size: length, 2¼" (57mm).

Habitat: Found around rocks, kelp, and on sponges, from 20' (6m) to 600' (182m).

Range: Arctic to Cape Cod. In the southern part of its range, *L. polaris* is found in deeper water.

Comments: Like other shrimp, this species has cryptic markings that allow it to blend with its environment.

DATE

LOCATION

DATE

LOCATION

DATE

LOCATION

GREENLAND SHRIMP *Lebbeus groenlandicus*

Identification: This large, sturdy shrimp is elongate and has a small, slender rostrum. There are four large teeth behind the eyes, on the back of the carapace. The abdomen bends down at the third segment. This shrimp is best identified by the pointed side plates of the abdominal segments. The last joint of the second walking leg has bead-like swellings. Color: variable—reddish, brownish, or brownish green; may be marbled or have irregular stripes. Size: length, 2¼" (57mm); height, 5/8" (16mm).

Habitat: Found around rocks and kelp beds, from low-tide line to 700' (212m).

Range: Arctic to Massachusetts.

Comments: The Greenland Shrimp is thicker and more full-bodied than Montague's Shrimp, *Pandalus montagui.* The side plates of the Montague's abdominal segments are rounded below, not pointed like those of the Greenland Shrimp.

Greenland Shrimp color variation

HAIRY HERMIT CRAB *Pagurus arcuatus*

Identification: As the name implies, this hermit crab is very hairy. The abdomen is asymmetrical, with a twist that gives it the ability to hold itself in a gastropod shell. The second antennae and eyes are on long stalks. The outer face of the chela is convex, and it has a central ridge of spines along the minor chela of the first left leg. Color: brown, changing to orange on the appendages. Size: to 1½" (37mm).

Habitat: Found on rocky bottoms, subtidally to 600' (180m).

Range: Arctic to Long Island.

Comments: This is primarily a northern hermit crab.

DATE

LOCATION

DATE

LOCATION

DATE

LOCATION

FLAT-CLAWED HERMIT CRAB *Pagurus pollicaris*

Identification: The main (right-hand) claw on this large hermit is broad and flat; it has many tubercles, and there is a projecting angle on the pincer. The left claw lacks this projecting angle. The carapace is wider at the rear; the cephalothorax is hard and flat. The first pair of antennae is shorter than the second. Color: gray, tan, or reddish. Size: length, 1¼" (31mm); width, 1" (25mm).

Habitat: Found on sandy bottoms, from shallow water to 360' (109m).

Range: Cape Cod to Texas, but some have been reported as far north as Maine.

Comments: Often found in the shells of large whelks and moon snails. When the crab has withdrawn into its shell, the large claw remains outside and serves as a barrier by blocking the entrance. The Zebra Flatworm, *Stylochus ellipticus,* is often found living commensally within the shell. This animal is also known as the Shield Hermit Crab.

ACADIAN HERMIT CRAB *Pagurus acadianus*

Identification: Like others in the family Paguridae, this species has a hard, flat carapace on the cephalothorax. The first pair of legs have pincers with an orange stripe down the middle and are covered with tubercles; the right leg is much bigger. The next two pairs of legs are longer; the fourth and the fifth pairs are shorter, with the fifth pair curling upward. Color: carapace—brown; legs—red-orange to brown, white at the base; first pair of antennae and eye stalks—blue; eyes—yellow. Size: carapace—length, 1¼" (31mm); width, 1" (25mm).

Habitat: On gravel or rocky bottoms; found in tide pools in the northern part of its range, to 1,600' (485m) in the southern part of its range.

Range: Arctic to Chesapeake Bay.

Comments: The last appendages have adapted to secure this crustacean in the shell that it occupies. The Long-clawed Hermit Crab, *Pagurus longicaris,* is similar but lacks the hair on the legs that *P. acadianus* has. The two species are not often found together.

Close-up of Acadian Hermit Cra

DATE

LOCATION

DATE

LOCATION

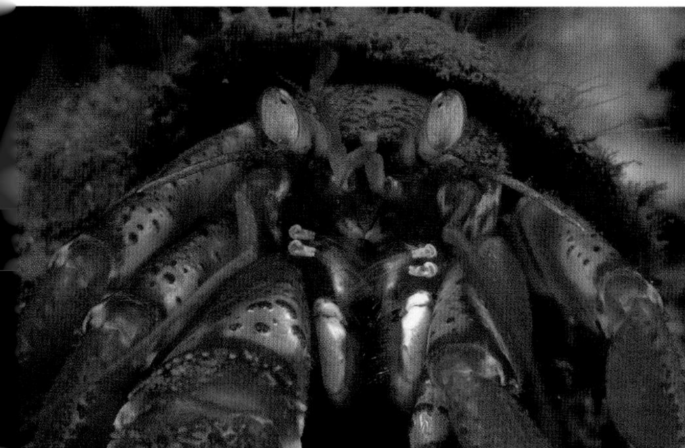

DATE

LOCATION

NORTHERN LOBSTER *Homarus americanus*

Identification: This large arthropod is easy to identify. The body is comprised of two main parts, the cylindrical cephalothorax (head/thorax) and the abdomen (tail section). The left pincer is usually larger and more stout, with rounded teeth; the right pincer is thinner, sharp, and pointed. The head has two pairs of antennae (the second is very long) and one pair of eyes on short, flexible stalks. The first three pairs of walking legs have pincers. The six segments of the tail have swimmerets, and the first two pairs on the male are modified for copulation. The telson, a broad fin at the end of the tail, is used by the lobster to propel itself in reverse. Color: greenish brown or orangish, but may be blue, white, or red. Size: length, to 4' (1.2m); height, to 9" (23cm).

Habitat: Found on rocky and sandy bottoms, from shallow water to 2,000' (606m).

Range: Labrador to North Carolina.

Comments: The Northern Lobster is nocturnal and prefers to live in crevices during the daytime. It feeds on crabs, sea stars, urchins, worms, and other animals found on the bottom. The heavier pincer is used for crushing the prey, while the lighter pincer is used for tearing or cutting the food. In the summer these scavengers migrate to inshore waters, and many are caught in traps that are baited with dead fish. Larger individuals are able to migrate hundreds of miles in a summer. With the onset of winter storms, they return to deeper water.

Lobsters, like other arthropods, grow by shedding their exoskeleton and increase in size as the new one forms. During the time that the exoskeleton needs to harden (ten days), they are very vulnerable to predation and are the favorite food of fish such as cod, haddock, goosefish, striped bass, and sharks. They molt as many as ten times in the first year; after the fourth year they molt only once a year. In the warm waters south of Cape Cod, they molt twice a year.

The bright orange eggs are carried under the female's abdomen and hatch between May and October. Lobsters can live to a hundred years and can reach 45 pounds (20.5 kg)! This arthropod is more closely related to freshwater crayfish than to any local marine crustaceans.

The lobster has a very interesting history. Native Americans used the plentiful crustaceans as fertilizer, and the early colonists considered them food for the poor.

Northern Lobster

Northern Lobster in a crevice, a common daytime location

DATE

LOCATION

DATE

LOCATION

DATE

LOCATION

COMMON SPIDER CRAB *Libinia emarginata*

Identification: The carapace of this crab is oval with a row of nine spines down the midline of the upper surface. The carapace also has many other smaller spines and hairs, and it is often covered with debris and small invertebrates. The rostrum is triangular, with a small fork. Color: grayish to brown. Size: carapace, 4" (10cm); legs, span to 1' (30cm).

Habitat: Found on various types of bottoms, especially mud, from low tide to 160' (48m), some have been found as deep as 400' (120m).

Range: Nova Scotia to Gulf of Mexico.

Comments: When *L. emarginata* climbs out from under the sand, its long legs give it the appearance of a giant spider. The walking legs of the male are almost twice as long as those of the female.

Similar Species: *L. dubina* is similar in size but has six spines on its back, and its rostrum is deeply forked.

TOAD CRAB *Hyas coarctatus*

Identification: Each side of the carapace has an indentation that gives the crab a violin shape. The rostrum is divided into two sections that have a narrow split between them. The carapace features a large projection behind the eye. The pincers are small. Color: reddish orange to brownish. Size: length, 2" (51mm); width, 1¼" (32mm).

Habitat: Found among rocks, on mud bottoms, or on kelp; from the low-tide line to 170' (52m).

Range: Arctic to Cape Hatteras.

Similar species: The Toad Crab, *H. araneus,* is larger and lacks an indentation (in the carapace) as deep as that in *H. coarctatus.* Moreover, the projection of the carapace behind the eye is more prominent in *H. coarctatus.* Older individuals of both species are often covered with algae, bryozoans, or coralline algae, making positive identification difficult.

The Toad Crab often has organisms growing on its carapace

DATE

LOCATION

DATE

LOCATION

DATE

LOCATION

ROCK CRAB *Cancer irroratus*

Identification: The carapace is broad, convex, and inundated with fine granulations. The forward border of the carapace has nine rounded, successively-pointed teeth with granulated edges. Between each tooth, there is a short groove on the carapace. Color: carapace—yellowish with many brick red to purple red or purplish brown dots. Size: carapace width, to 5" (127mm).

Habitat: Found on rocky shores, intertidally to 2,600' (780m).

Range: Arctic to South Carolina.

Comments: A very common crab in the intertidal area. Highly edible; provides the crabmeat widely available in Maine.

Similar Species: The Jonah Crab, *C. borealis,* has jagged, marginal teeth.

Male Atlantic Rock Crab holding on to the female, which releases a pheromone to attract the male. He carries her for weeks in order to mate when she has molted. At the same time, he provides her with protection because her shell is soft and defenseless.

(Left) Female Atlantic Rock Crab "standing on toes" as the eggs hatch into larvae and are released into the water. The eggs become brownish as they are about to hatch.

(Bottom, right) Female Atlantic Rock Crab holds onto eggs (orange), under her abdomen, with appendages

DATE

LOCATION

DATE

LOCATION

DATE

LOCATION

JONAH CRAB *Cancer borealis*

Identification: The carapace is oval-shaped, and its surface is finely granular. There are three low teeth between the eyes and nine wide teeth with deep, indented margins on each side of the eye socket. The walking legs are short and hairy with black tips. Color: carapace—brick red, ventral surface—yellowish. Size: length, 4" (102mm); width, 6" (156mm).

Habitat: Rocky shores and bottoms, intertidally to 2,600' (800m).

Range: Nova Scotia to Florida.

Comments: Also known as Northern Crab. It can be confused with *C. irroratus,* but the carapace of the *C. irroratus* has a sharp point at the widest part.

GREEN CRAB *Carcinus maenas*

Identification: The carapace of this fan-shaped crab is wider than it is long. There are three frontal teeth, along with five on either side of the eye socket. The last pair of legs is pointed and somewhat flattened, but not paddle-like as are those of the Lady Crab. The carapace of the males is green, and the ventral side is yellowish. The females are orange red ventrally. Size: carapace width, to 3" (76mm).

Habitat: Among rocks, intertidally to shallow water.

Range: Nova Scotia to New Jersey.

Comments: This common crab delights many visitors at tide pools. Easily attracted to dead fish or crushed shellfish. The green crab is not an indigenous species. It was probably introduced via bilge water from foreign vessels.

Green Crab

DATE

LOCATION

DATE

LOCATION

DATE

LOCATION

BLUE CRAB *Callinectes sapidus*

Identification: At least twice as wide as it is long, the smooth carapace of the Blue Crab is spindle-shaped, with a very large, sharp, lateral spine. On the carapace there are four triangular teeth between the eyes and eight strong, pointed teeth between the eye socket and the large lateral spine. The last pair of walking legs is paddle-shaped (modified for swimming). The large claws have three spines on the first segment. Color: carapace—greenish above, whitish underneath; legs—blue; pincers—male, blue; female, red. Size: width, 9" (227mm); length, 4" (102mm).

Habitat: Found in shallow water and brackish estuaries, subtidally to 120' (37m).

Range: Cape Cod to Uruguay; has been reported in Nova Scotia.

Comments: The Blue Crab is an important commercial shellfish. "Soft-shell" crab is really a blue crab that has been kept in a pen, allowed to molt, and then harvested. (In the wild, recently molted crabs would be found hiding in a protected place.) It is then fried and consumed entirely. The Blue Crab is a fast swimmer and a voracious carnivore that is often able to catch small fish. It will even nip at the toes of people wading in the shallow water. In the Chesapeake Bay the males are called Jimmies, Channelers, or Jimmy-dicks. Young females are known as Sally Crabs, and adult females are called Sooks. The female dies within a year after spawning.

LADY CRAB *Ovalipes ocellatus*

Identification: The carapace is somewhat wider than it is long. It has five marginal teeth on either side of the eyes. The chelipeds are long in proportion to their width. The pincers are serrated, sharp, and very long. The walking legs are flat. The last pair of legs are paddle-like and allow the crab to swim well. Color: carapace—light gray to lavender with purple speckles. Size: 3" (76mm).

Habitat: On sand, mud, or rock bottoms, from the low-tide line to 150' (46m). In winter, it goes to the deeper water.

Range: Cape Cod to Gulf of Mexico and around Prince Edward Island.

Comments: This beautiful swimming crab, also known as the Calico Crab, is aggressive and quick.

Lady Crab swimming

DATE

LOCATION

DATE

LOCATION

DATE

LOCATION

SAND FIDDLER *Uca pugilator*

Identification: The carapace of the male is somewhat square. The upper surface is purple or slate colored, with irregular dark markings. The female is almost rectangular, is darker than the male, and lacks the rasping ridge of the inside claw. The eye stalks are long and thin. Size: carapace, 1" (25mm). The male has one claw that is very large, up to 1¼" (38mm).

Habitat: Sandy or muddy beaches, especially up near the high-tide line.

Range: Cape Cod to Texas.

Comments: The oversized claw of the male is used for courtship displays and as a threat to other males. It is actually quite harmless. The fiddler burrows underground and carries from its lair small scoops of sand, which it deposits near the opening. As you walk toward a group of these crabs, they quickly scurry into their well maintained burrows. Sand Fiddlers feed on algae and decaying marsh grass. Also called Calico-backed Fiddler.

Similar Species: The Mud Fiddler, *Uca pugnax,* and the Brackish-water Fiddler, (Red-jointed Fiddler), *Uca minax.*

Sand Fiddler coming out of its burrow

Male Sand Fiddler with larger right claw

DATE

LOCATION

DATE

LOCATION

DATE

LOCATION

ECHINODERMATA

Echinoderms have relatives in all marine habitats, ranging from estuaries to great ocean depths. There are six thousand known species of echinoderms. All are strictly marine and dwell on the bottom of the ocean. Members of this phylum are some of the most familiar marine invertebrates. An animal such as the sea star is a common icon of sea life.

Echinoderms have a body design completely different from that seen in any other phylum. The body plan features radial symmetry, with the components generally arranged in five sections, or multiples thereof, around a central axis. There is an internal, limy skeleton that generally has projecting spines or tubercles. These give its surface a warty or spiny appearance. The words "echino" (spine) and "derm" (skin) describe these animals well. Although some representatives have sharper spines, most have rounded, calcareous projections or fine, hair-like extensions that cover the skin of the animal. In Sea Cucumbers, the skin can be smooth or warty.

Echinoderms have a well-developed water vascular system, which is used for movement and predation. This system is characterized by contractile tube feet and a madreporite. The madreporite, also called the sieve plate, connects the vascular system to water outside the animal. Tube feet are arranged in rows on the body. Water is pumped to the tube feet to extend them, and muscles within the tube feet can retract them. The animal can move efficiently by holding onto rocks or substrate with the suction of the tube feet. As a feeding mechanism in sea stars, arms with tube feet enclose a clam or mussel and exert pressure until the muscle of the bivalve can no longer hold it closed.

Reproduction is sexual in all species. Sexes are indistinguishable but separate. Usually, an environmental condition signals the release of eggs or sperm into the water, resulting in free-swimming larval forms. In some species, such as the polar star, eggs may be brooded by the adults. Regeneration of appendages is characteristic of some echinoderms.

Three classes are common in our North Atlantic waters. Stelleroidea (stars), Echinoidea (sea urchins and sand dollars), and Holothuroidea (sea cucumbers) can be found from the intertidal zone to very deep water. The fourth class, Crinoidea (sea lilies and feather stars), are found in deeper water (100 meters or more) and in tropical waters.

Sea Star

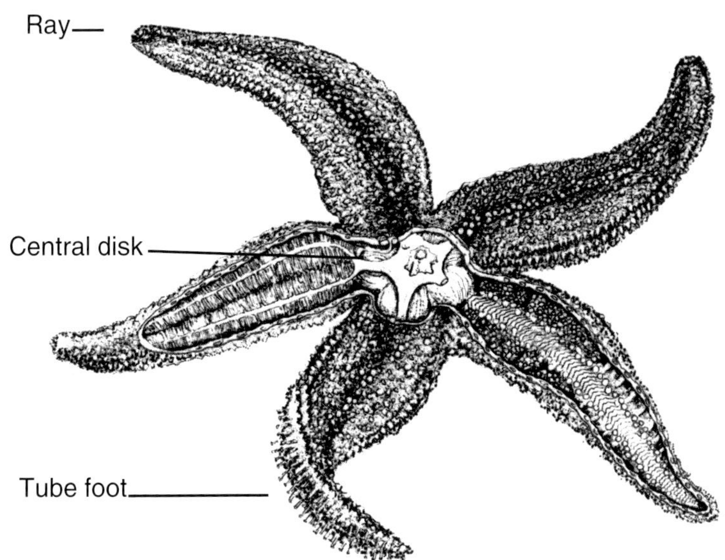

Brittle Star

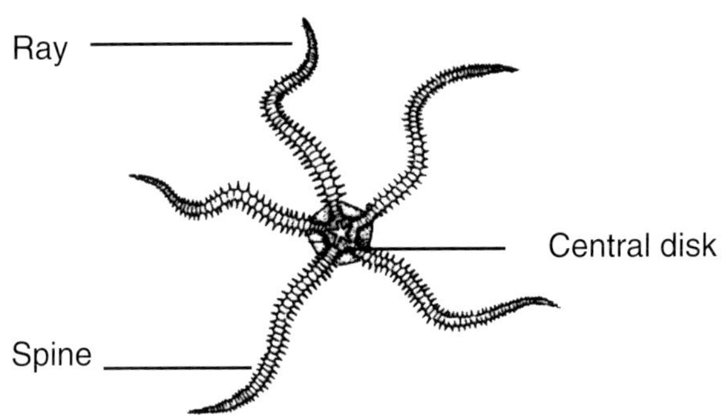

Sea Urchin

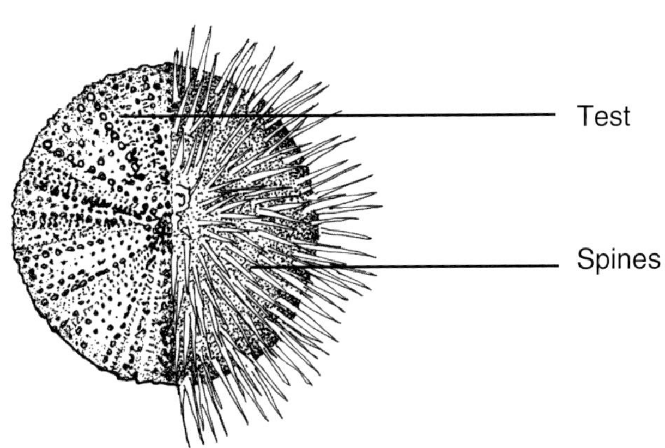

Echinoderms/Holothurians

SCARLET PSOLUS *Psolus fabricii*

Identification: This sea cucumber is oval shaped and has a flat bottom that adheres to the solid substrate. The dorsal and lateral sides are covered with a tile-like outer surface. The mouth is located at one end of the dorsal surface, and the anus is on the other. Around the mouth are ten tentacles. Each immediately divides into three branches, all of which continue to subdivide until a network of fine tentacles is formed. The anus, equipped with five anal teeth, is on a cone but does not project as much as the mouth. Tube feet are found around the margin of the sole. Color: scarlet to orange. Size: to 8" (20cm).

Habitat: Found on rocks, subtidally to 1,300' (394m).

Range: Arctic to Cape Cod.

Comments: This is a fascinating animal to watch as it feeds. *P. fabricii* spreads its arms into the water column in order to snare particles of food that pass by. In a random pattern, one arm at a time is placed into the mouth, where the food is removed. As the arm pulls out of the mouth, it is recoated with a sticky mucus that enables it to capture more food. At the same time, another arm is getting ready to enter the mouth. This pattern will continue for a long time and will delight anyone who is fortunate enough to witness this spectacle.

Scarlet Psolus places an arm (located at two o'clock) into its mouth

(Left) Scarlet Psolus coats the tentacles with mucus as it withdraws its arm from its mouth

(Bottom, right) Scarle Psolus opens its mouth an places an arm (located a eleven o'clock) in its mout

DATE

LOCATION

DATE

LOCATION

DATE

LOCATION

Echinoderms/Holothurians

ORANGE-FOOTED CUCUMBER *Cucumaria frondosa*

Identification: The body is cucumber-shaped, with thick, leathery skin and five longitudinal, radial rows of tube feet. At one end, there are ten branching, tree-like, retractable tentacles that surround the mouth. The tube feet are also retractable and can be used to help manipulate the body. Color: body and tentacles, reddish brown, occasionally pink to whitish; tube feet, brown to orange. Size: length, 19" (48cm); width, 5" (127mm).

Habitat: Found on rocks and other hard substrate, intertidally to 1,200' (364m).

Range: Arctic to Cape Cod.

Comments: This is the largest and most common sea cucumber in New England. It feeds on plankton by extending its arms into the water. As the mucus-coated arms catch the plankton, they are put one by one into the mouth, where the food is removed and the arms are recoated with mucus.

(Middle, left) Orange-footed Cucumber putting an arm (located at nine o'clock) into its mouth

(Middle, right) Orange-footed Cucumber putting a different arm (located at three o'clock) into its mouth

---

BROWN PSOLUS *Psolus phantapus*

Identification: This psolus is often found protruding from the sand or mud. The dorsal side has a dome shaped outline. The anterior end is turned upward with a mouth and crown of 10 branching tentacles. The posterior end also turns upwards, tapers like an erected tail and has the anal opening at the tip. Tentacles are sparsely branched. The ventral side is almost rectangular. Color: body, dull reddish orange to reddish brown with scales outlined in a darker brown; tentacles, mottled brown to reddish brown. Size: 6" (156mm).

Habitat: Found in sand or gravel bottom with only the top half protruding from the sand.

Range: Arctic to Cape Cod. It is also found in Great Britain.

Comments: It is preyed upon by cod and the large sunstars.

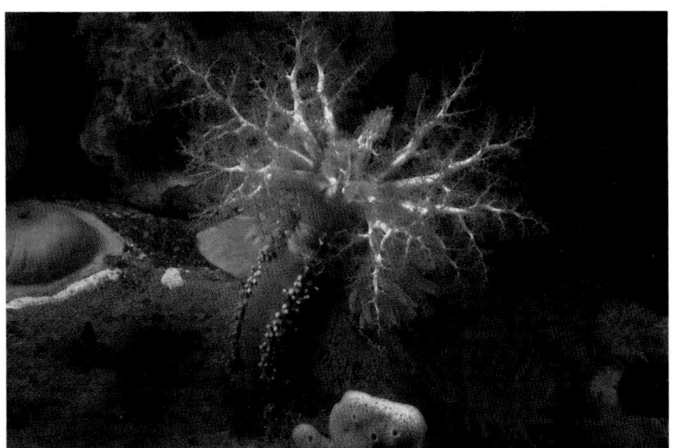

DATE

LOCATION

DATE

LOCATION

HAIRY SEA CUCUMBER *Sclerodactyla briareus*

Identification: Covered with slender tube feet, the body is oval shaped and tapers toward the posterior. The ends of the mouth and tail are bent upward. There are ten large, tree-like tentacles; the two lowest are smaller. Color: brownish, olive, blackish, and purplish. Size: length, 4¾" (121mm); width, 2" (51mm).

Habitat: Found on sandy or muddy bottoms, from the low-tide line to 20' (6m).

Range: Cape Cod to the Gulf of Mexico.

Comments: The Hairy Sea Cucumber buries itself in the soft substrate, exposing only the tentacles, mouth, and anus. It can regenerate lost tentacles in three weeks.

SILKY SEA CUCUMBER *Chiridota laevis*

Identification: This cucumber is worm-like, smooth, and lacking tube feet. There are twelve tentacles, each of which has a cluster of ten short, finger-like branches. Color: transparent white to pink. Size: length, 6" (15cm); width, 1/2" (13mm).

Habitat: Found under rocks, subtidally to 270' (82m).

Range: Arctic to Cape Cod.

PURPLE SEA URCHIN *Arbacia punctulata*

Identification: The test is covered with cylindrical, rigid spines that vary in size on different parts of the body. The periproct, the large central opening used for the anus, is on top of the test and has few spines around it. The peristome (the mouth) is centrally located on the bottom of the test. Color: purple to reddish brown. Size: to 2" (51mm). The largest spines (near the top) can reach 1" (25mm).

Habitat: On rocky or shell bottom, from the low-tide line to 700' (212m); a common sight in tide pools, rock crevices, and seaweed beds.

Range: Cape Cod to Gulf of Mexico.

Comments: *A. punctulata* has longer spines than the Green Sea Urchin. The Purple Sea Urchin is omnivorous, feeding on sponges, algae, other invertebrates, and dead animals.

DATE

LOCATION

DATE

LOCATION

DATE

LOCATION

GREEN SEA URCHIN *Stronglyocentrotus droebachiensis*

Identification: This small sea urchin has spines that are not more than one-third the width of its test. There are no spines on the plates of the periproct (anus), which is located at the midpoint, on the top of the test. Made up of small plates, the test is wider than it is tall and has a broad arch underneath. The tube feet are long and extend far beyond the tips of the spines. Color: test—greenish brown, spines—green, tube feet—brown. Size: width, 3¼" (82mm); height, 1½" (38mm).

Habitat: Found on rocky bottoms, in tide pools, and in kelp beds; intertidally to 3,800' (1254m).

Range: Arctic to New Jersey.

Comments: This urchin feeds on algae and can reduce a kelp bed to just stubs in a short time. In recent years, *S. droebachiensis* has become commercially important. The roe, a delicacy, is exported to Japan. The Green Sea Urchin is the dominant species north of Cape Cod, whereas the Purple Sea Urchin, *Arbacia punctulata,* is the common urchin south of the Cape.

Green Sea Urchin releasing its yellow eggs

Green Sea Urchin uses its tube feet for locomotion and to hold on to the substrate

DATE

LOCATION

DATE

LOCATION

DATE

LOCATION

COMMON SAND DOLLAR *Echinarachnius parma*

Identification: This flat echinoid is circular and has a very thin test, with a five-point, petal-like pattern of tiny holes on its upper surface. The mouth—located underneath, in the center—has five branching grooves leading to it. The anal opening is at the edge of the test. Color: reddish purple and brownish. Size: width, 3⅛" (79mm); height, 1/4" (6mm).

Habitat: Found on sandy bottoms, from the low-tide line to 1 mile (1,613m) deep.

Range: Labrador to Maryland.

Comments: Feeds on minute particles of organic material. Sand Dollars are preyed upon by ocean pout, flounder, cod, and other bottom feeders. The white tests are often found on beaches after storms. The purplish color of the live Sand Dollar is very soluble and stains indelibly.

Sand Dollar moves along the bottom

Sand Dollar test (left) and live animal (right)

DATE

LOCATION

DATE

LOCATION

DATE

LOCATION

SMOOTH SUNSTAR *Solaster endeca*

Identification: This large sea star usually has nine to ten arms but can be found with seven to fourteen arms. The upper surface is covered with short paxillae and very short spines. Color: reddish, pink, yellow, purple, or deep violet red with yellow margins; madreporite—light yellow. Size: radius, 8" (20cm).

Habitat: Found on rocky bottoms, subtidally to 900' (273m).

Range: Arctic to Cape Cod.

Comments: This sunstar feeds on invertebrates and small sea stars. As in the Spiny Sunstar, there is no free-swimming larval stage; it develops directly from the egg. Also known as Purple Sunstar.

Smooth Sunstar color variation

More color variations in the Smooth Sunstar

DATE

LOCATION

DATE

LOCATION

SPINY SUNSTAR *Crossaster papposus*

Identification: This beautiful sunstar usually has from ten to twelve arms but can be found with eight to fourteen. The upper surface is covered with bristles, the longest ones on the arms. Underneath are two rows of tube feet in the grooves of each arm. The central disc is large. Color: upper side—red with white or red concentric bands; underside—whitish. Size: radius, 7" (175mm).

Habitat: Found on rocky bottoms, subtidally to 1,000' (303m).

Range: Arctic to New Jersey.

Comments: Likened to a star burst, this echinoderm is a voracious predator that feeds on many invertebrates, such as mollusks, sea anemones, and other sea stars. It has no free-swimming larval stage and develops directly from the egg.

A close-up of Spiny Sunstar shows the spines that are present on the projections (pseudopaxillae)

Spiny Sunstar color variation

DATE

LOCATION

DATE

LOCATION

DATE

LOCATION

BLOOD SEA STAR *Henricia sanguinolenta*

Identification: This colorful little sea star has a small disc and five slender, cylindrical, pointed arms of equal length. On the surface are small, equal-sized spines that form a fine granular covering. There are two rows of tube feet. Color: variable—red, orange, yellow, white, purple, and mottled. Size: radius, 4" (102mm).

Habitat: Found on rocky bottoms, from the low-tide line to 7,920' (2414m).

Range: Arctic to Cape Hatteras.

Comments: *H. sanguinolenta* feeds on sponges. Different from other sea stars, it can absorb nutrients through its outer surface. The Blood Star broods its eggs and, therefore, has no free-swimming larval stage. The eggs are deposited around the mouth, and the arms are gathered to form a brood pouch. In this protected area, the eggs can develop into tiny sea stars that are eventually able to live on their own.

Blood Star feeding on a Palmate Sponge

(Bottom, left) A Blood Star that has regenerated a sixth arm

(Bottom, right) Blood Star color variatio

DATE

LOCATION

DATE

LOCATION

FORBES' SEA STAR *Asterias forbesi*

Identification: This common species usually has five arms, though it can be found with four to seven. These are stout, almost cylindrical, and blunt at the tips. The central disc is moderate in size and often somewhat dome shaped. The upper surface is rough, with spines of various sizes and small pincer-like pedicellariae. Underneath are four rows of tube feet. Color: variable—tones of brown, orange, red, purple, and green; madreporite—often orange. Size: radius, 5" (127mm).

Habitat: Found intertidally on rocky, sandy, and gravelly bottoms to 150' (45m).

Range: Generally from Massachusetts to Texas, but can also be found as far north as Maine.

Comments: *Asterias forbesi* releases free-floating eggs into the water column. It is interesting to watch these sea stars "stand" on the tips of their arms and release the eggs from the top. Feeding mainly on bivalves, this creature exerts a constant force on the sides of the shell (10 to 15 lbs/sq. inch) until the mollusk begins to fatigue. This sea star needs an opening of only 1/250" (.1mm) to feed. It everts its stomach through its own mouth, inserts it into the bivalve, and secretes digestive juices into the mollusk until the creature dies. Then it absorbs the liquid meal that forms within the shells of the bivalve. This voracious sea star has always been a problem in oyster beds.

Similar species: *Asterias vulgaris* looks very similar but has a row of spines down the middle of the upper surface of each arm. In addition, its madreporite is yellowish.

The tube feet of a Forbes' Sea Star

(Bottom, left) A Forbes' Sea Star that has regenerated a sixth arm

(Bottom, right) A Forbes' Sea Star regenerating three arms

DATE

LOCATION

DATE

LOCATION

NORTHERN SEA STAR *Asterias vulgaris*

Identification: This common sea star usually has five flattened arms that taper to a narrow tip. The central disc is large. The upper surface has many pincer-like pedicellariae and is covered with short, blunt spines. The madreporite is pale yellow and smaller than that of *A. forbesi*. There is often a row of spines down the middle of the upper surface of the arm. Their underside has blunt spines and four rows of tube feet (a characteristic of Asteriid stars). Color—variable, shades of red, purple, orange, brown, and green. Size: radius, 8" (20cm).

Habitat: Similar to Forbes' Sea Star, *Asterias forbesi,* but can be found down to 2,000' (600m).

Range: Labrador to Cape Hatteras; more common north of Cape Cod than Forbes' Sea Star.

Comments: Also known as Common Sea Star (starfish).

Similar species: Forbes' Seastar, *A. forbesi*; Slender Green Seastar, *Leptasterias littoralis*; Polar Sea Star, *L. polaris*; and Slender Seastar, *L. tenera.*

Northern Sea Star releasing eggs from the top of its central disc

(Bottom, left) Northern Sea Star feeding on Blue Mussel

(Bottom, right) A Northern Sea Star regenerating four arms

DATE

LOCATION

DATE

LOCATION

POLAR SEA STAR *Leptasterias polaris*

Identification: The Polar Sea Star is similar in shape to the Northern Sea Star, *Asterias vulgaris,* but it has six arms. There are four rows of tube feet on each arm, and the skin has small pincer-like pedicellariae that may be clustered or scattered. Color: variable—tan, greenish, yellowish, and mottled. Size: radius, 5" (127mm).

Habitat: Found on rocky bottoms, subtidally to 1,200' (364m).

Range: Gulf of St. Lawrence to Maine.

Comments: The Polar Sea Star, like other Leptasterias stars, broods its eggs and does not have a free-swimming larval stage.

A Polar Sea Star placing its arms in a circle to brood its eggs

---

GREEN SLENDER SEA STAR *Leptasterias littoralis*

Identification: Similar to the Northern Sea Star, *Asterias vulgaris,* except that its arms are more slender. The upper surface is rough, with a conspicuous row of thin spines (there are no clearly-defined row of spines on the arms). Color: upper surface—greenish, madreporite—white. Size: radius, 1½" (37mm).

Habitat: Intertidally to shallow water, on hard bottoms and Fucus-covered rocks.

Range: Arctic to Gulf of Maine.

Comments: Members of this genus are brooders. The female carries her eggs and recently-hatched young in a brood sac near the mouth.

DATE

LOCATION

DATE

LOCATION

DATE

LOCATION

WINGED SEA STAR *Pteraster militaria*

Identification: The Winged Sea Star has a large disc, thick body, and blunt arms. As in other stars of this family (Pterasteridae), its body is surrounded by a wing-like membrane (supported by spines) instead of marginal plates. There are two rows of tube feet in the grooves under each arm. There is a pair of strong spines on the surface near the five jaws that surround the mouth. Color: upper surface—yellowish or reddish, underside—tan or white. Size: radius, 2¾" (70mm).

Habitat: Found on rocky bottoms, subtidally to 3,600' (1091m).

Range: Arctic to Cape Cod.

Comments: With the aid of its wing-like membrane, the Winged Sea Star forms a pouch to brood its eggs, which remain there until they become little stars and are able to push through the protective membrane. This species is also called Cushion Sea Star.

Winged Sea Star color variation

A Winged Sea Star that has regenerated a sixth arm

DATE

LOCATION

DATE

LOCATION

DATE

LOCATION

BADGE STAR *Porania insignis*

Identification: This blunt-armed star is easily recognized by the thick skin that covers its upper surface. There are two rows of tube feet extending from the center of the disc to the tips of the arms. Color: upper surface—red with white markings in the creases of the skin, underside—white, sieve plate—white. Size: radius, 2¾" (70mm).

Habitat: Found on rocky bottoms, from 90' to 2,200' (27 to 666m).

Range: Massachusetts Bay to Cape Hatteras.

Comments: Feeds on small organic matter that adheres to its mucus-covered body. Cilia on the star's surface move the food to the mouth.

HORSE STAR *Hippasteria phrygiana*

Identification: This rigid sea star is almost pentagonal. The upper surface has large rounded spines that are encircled by smaller, beaded spines. On the underside, there are also two rows of tube feet. There are also large pedicellariae that look like small bivalves on both surfaces. Color: red above and whitish underneath. Size: radius, 8" (20cm).

Habitat: Found on rocky bottoms, from 30' (9m) to over 2,000' (606m).

Range: Arctic to Cape Cod.

Comment: This carnivore feeds on bivalves, echinoderms, and worms. Its spiny surface makes it easy to recognize.

The underside of a Horse Sta

DATE
LOCATION
DATE
LOCATION
DATE
LOCATION

Echinoderms/Ophiuroids

NORTHERN BASKET STAR *Gorgonocephalus arcticus*

Identification: This beautiful star has five stout, cylindrical arms that originate from the central disc and branch repeatedly, forming V-shaped divisions. Five pairs of spiny rows radiate from the large, pentagonal, naked, central disc to the sides of the arms. Color: upper surface of disc—brown to yellowish brown; underside—white; arms—tan, but white at the tips. Size: disc diameter, 4" (102mm); arm length, 14" (36cm).

Habitat: Found on rocky bottoms, from 18' (6m) to 4,831' (1472m).

Range: Arctic to Cape Cod.

Comments: The Northern Basket Star uses its lower arms to support itself and extends its other arms into the water to feed. At other times the arms are coiled and interwoven, which gives the star the appearance of a basket. Small basket stars are often seen perched on Red Soft Coral, *Gersemia rubiformis.* At times, several Northern Basket Stars connect to each other and form into a large net. This allows them to work together and feed on larger animals.

(Right) a juvenile Northern Basket Star on Red Soft Coral

(Left) A Northern Basket Star extends its arms to gather food

(Right, bottom) A Northern Basket Star with its arms withdrawn and coiled

DATE

LOCATION

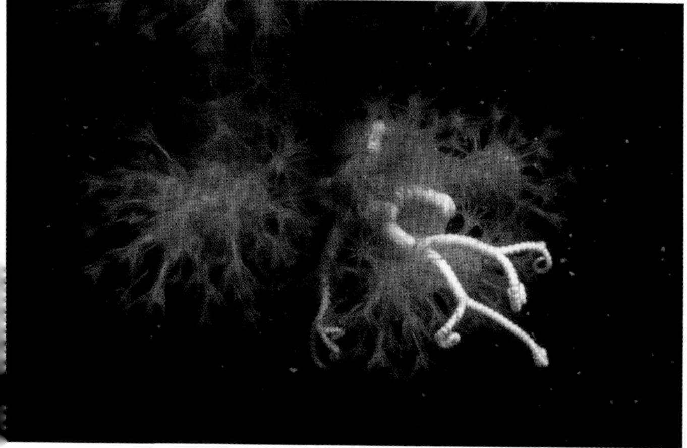

DATE

LOCATION

DATE

LOCATION

DAISY BRITTLE STAR *Ophiopholis aculeata*

Identification: The scalloped disc of this brittle star is covered with small spines that conceal the scales but not the large, oval plates. The lobes of the disc extend between the arms, which have five to six lateral spines on each joint. Color: variable—countless combinations of yellow, orange, red, black, green, tan, gray, and brown; may be banded, spotted, or mottled. Size: disc diameter, 3/4" (18mm); arm length, 3½" (88mm).

Habitat: Found under rocks, in kelp holdfasts, and in crevices; intertidally to 5,000' (1500m).

Range: Arctic to Cape Cod.

Comments: In the daytime, all you will generally see of this small star is a portion of the arms, because it is hiding from predators. At night it comes out to feed. The name is appropriate—the arms will break off easily if the animal is mishandled.

A Daisy Brittle Star with an arm broken off

A Daisy Brittle Star as it is commonly seen in the daytime, with only the arms visible

DATE

LOCATION

DATE

LOCATION

DATE

LOCATION

CHORDATA
(Tunicates)

Invertebrate chordates, called tunicates or ascidians, are classified in the same phylum as fish, mammals, and other bony animals, but they are actually part of a separate subphylum, Urochordata. Tunicates are primitive relatives of vertebrate animals. At some point in their development, all chordates have these things in common: a notochord, which is a moveable, rod-like support; pharyngeal gill slits that are either kept throughout the animal's life or lost during embryonic development; and a dorsal nerve cord. Tunicates have all of these during their larval stage but lose them during their adult stage. This enables them to be categorized with other chordates.

The typical tunicate has a sac-like body enclosed in a tough yet flexible outer tunic, known as the test. It lives permanently attached to the substrate or buried in the soft bottom. The most familiar representatives of this group are the ascidians, or sea squirts. They are called this because they squirt water from siphons as a defense when they are touched. Some tunicates occur as individual animals (like the Sea Peach and Sea Vase), while other species are colonial animals (like the Golden Star Tunicate and White Crust Tunicate). In the colonial animals, individuals are called zooids. Individual zooids measure about 1/4" (6mm) across, but colonies range from 4" to 12".

Tunicates are primarily filter feeders, pulling water through the tunic and feeding on plankton filtered from the water trapped inside. Waste products are eliminated by sending filtered water through the siphons or the tunic.

Adult forms come in a variety of shapes and sizes. They can be cask-like, spindle shaped, sac-like masses of lobed, gelatinous tissue, or simply sheets of thin encrustations. They are all marine and, when not pelagic (like the salps and appendicularians), they can be found on a variety of substrates from wharf pilings to rocks, shells, and seaweeds. Tunicates can be attached to the substrate or be free swimming.

Reproduction can be either asexual or sexual. In some colonial tunicates, asexual reproduction takes place by means of budding. In most cases, adult tunicates are hermaphroditic. Eggs are released from the atrial siphon. Fertilization may take place in the water column or in the body cavity. Development of the larvae may take place in the water or within the adult animal. When they hatch, the larvae are tadpole shaped.

Most ascidians have a life span of one to three years, although colonies may survive for longer.

Tunicate

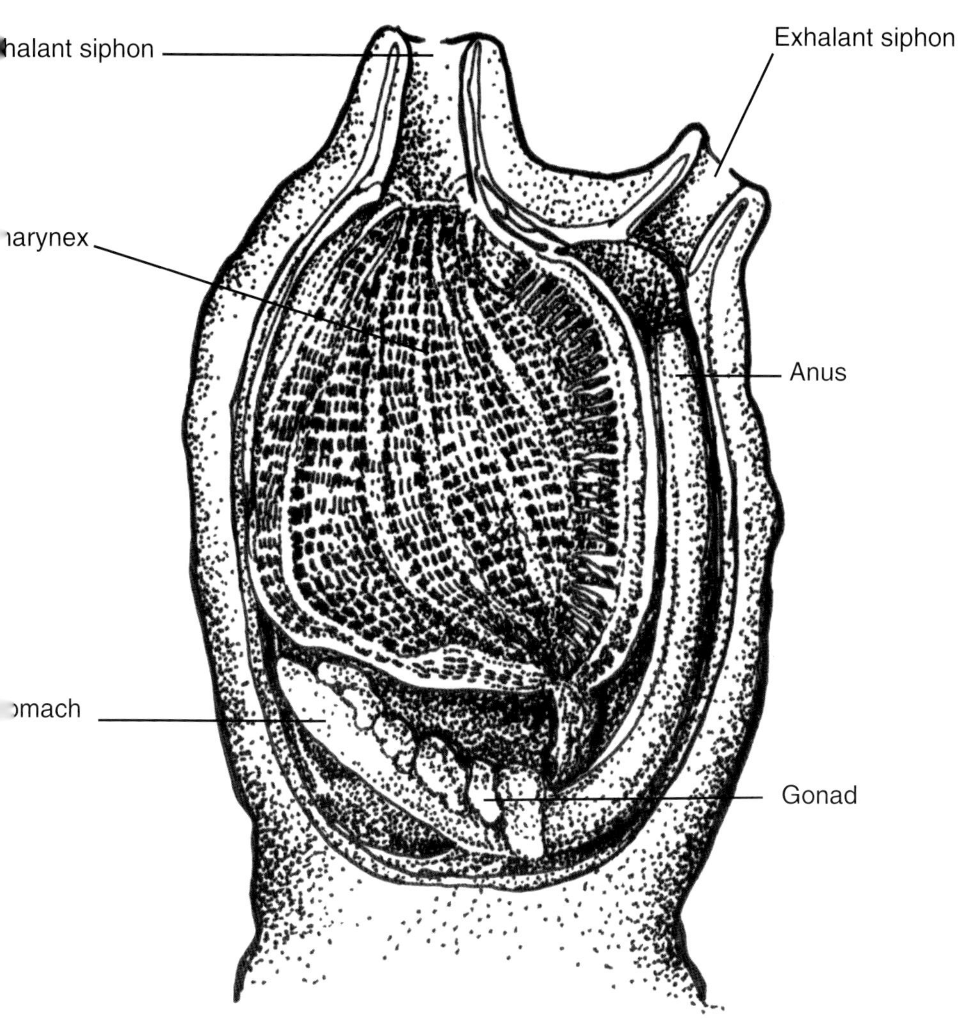

NORTHERN WHITE CRUST *Didemnum albidum*

Identification: The colonies of this tunicate form a low, white, irregular mass. The arrangement of the tiny zooids and the apertures is often irregular. There are minute calcareous spicules that make it opaque and quite hard and brittle. Color: white, pinkish, or yellowish. Size: width, 4" (102mm); height, 1/8" (3mm).

Habitat: Found on rocks, pilings, and other hard substrate, from the low-tide line to 1,350' (411m).

Range: Arctic to Cape Cod.

Similar species: Differentiating *D. albidum* from *D. candidum* requires the use of a microscope.

GOLDEN STAR TUNICATE *Botryllus schlosseri*

Identification: This encrusting colonial tunicate forms fleshy, loose rolls and lobes of varying thickness. The zooids are outlined in yellow or white. There are no spicules. Color: variable—black, brown, purple, olive, and yellow. Size: zooid—width, 1/16" (1.6mm); height,1/8" (3mm); colony—to 4" (102mm).

Habitat: Found on rocks, shells, wharf pilings, boat bottoms, algae, or any other solid surface.

Range: Bay of Fundy to North Carolina.

Comments: This is the most common colonial tunicate in the North Atlantic.

SEA GRAPE *Molgula* sp.

Identification: This tunicate is globular, grape-like, and often encrusted with debris. Siphons are dissimilar, one having four lobes and the other six. Size: 1" (25mm).

Habitat: Subtidal. Some Molgula species are found in the sand or mud, while others are attached to rocks, pilings and boat hulls.

Range: Arctic to North Carolina.

Comments: These are very common tunicates, able to live in a variety of water conditions. *Molgula manhattensis* can survive in a busy port like New York Harbor.

DATE

LOCATION

DATE

LOCATION

DATE

LOCATION

PINK SEA PORK *Amaroucium pellucidum*

Identification: This mass of cauliflower-like lobes houses many individuals in interconnected but inconspicuous clusters. It may be encrusted with sand. Color: pink to orange; some have whitish surfaces. Size: colonies, to 8" (20m).

Habitat: Found in shallow-water areas where there is a tidal current.

Range: Cape Cod to Gulf of Mexico.

Comments: This common tunicate also grows on wharf pilings.

(Right, top) Sea Pork

(Right, middle) Close-up of Sea Pork

STALKED TUNICATE *Boltenia ovifera*

Identification: Easy to identify, this creature has a stalk that is two to three times longer than its body, which may be smooth, wrinkled, or spiny. The siphons are on one side; the incurrent siphon is aimed upward, and the excurrent is aimed downward. Color: reddish orange, red, or tan. Size: body—height, 3" (76mm); width, 2" (51mm); stalk—length, 12" (30cm); width, 1/4" (6mm).

Habitat: Found on rocks, pilings, and other hard substrate, from the low-tide line to 1,640' (500m).

Range: Arctic to Cape Cod.

Comments: The body of the Stalked Tunicate is often covered with bryozoans, algae, and hydroids. It can be found as one or two animals alone or in large "fields" of tunicates covering 30 sq. ft. (10 sq. m).

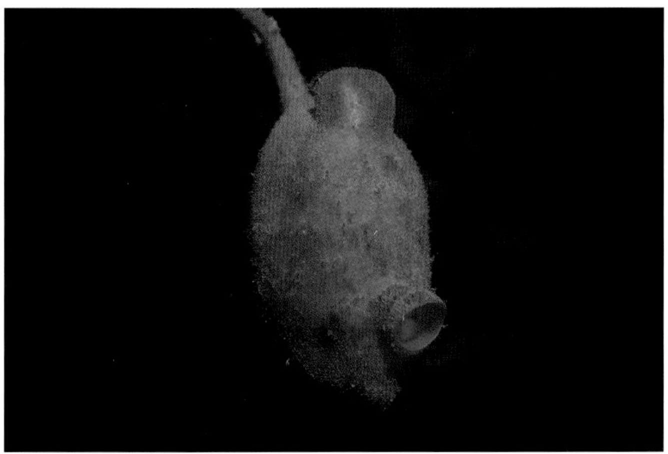

(Bottom, right) Stalked Tunicate

(Left) Close-up of Stalked Tunicate

DATE

LOCATION

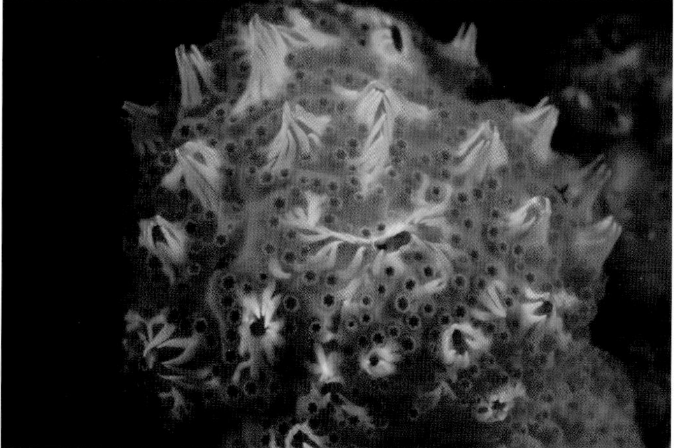

DATE

LOCATION

DATE

LOCATION

SEA VASE *Ciona intestinalis*

Identification: This tall and striking ascidian has five to seven muscle bands that are visible through its transparent test. It has two siphons. Water bearing food enters the branchial eight-lobed siphon (at right in picture) and exits the artial six-lobed siphon (at left in picture). Color: body, transparent or whitish; rims of the siphons, yellow. Size: height, 6" (15cm); width, 1" (25mm).

Habitat: On rocks, pilings, and other solid surfaces in shallow water.

Range: Arctic to Rhode Island.

Comments: This sea squirt is a common sight on pilings. Since it is so available, it has become the most thoroughly studied tunicate in the world. It pumps up to five gallons of water each day in the process of feeding and removing waste.

BLOOD DROP TUNICATE *Dendrodoa carnea*

Identification: The body is low, dome-shaped, and smooth. It has two short siphons and is attached to the substrate by its entire bottom surface. This tunicate does resemble a drop of blood. Color: red and pinkish. Size: width, 1/2" (12mm); height, 1/4" (6mm).

Habitat: Found on rocks, pilings, and other hard substrate, from the low-tide line to 250' (76m).

Range: Newfoundland to Long Island, New York.

Comments: The Blood Drop Tunicate is a brooder, and in late summer it releases red, tadpole-like larvae.

SEA PEACH *Halocynthia pyriformis*

Identification: The Sea Peach is a large, barrel-shaped tunicate in which both siphons have four lobes. The lower (excurrent) siphon is smaller. The surface is clean but like sandpaper. It is attached to the substrate by root-like strands. Color: orange and reddish yellow. Size: height, 5" (127mm); width, 3" (76mm).

Habitat: Found on rocks, pilings, and other hard substrate, from the low-tide line to 600' (182m).

Range: Arctic to Massachusetts Bay.

Comments: The largest specimens are found in the northern part of the animal's range.

DATE

LOCATION

DATE

LOCATION

DATE

LOCATION

CLUB TUNICATE *Styela clava*

Identification: This tunicate is warty, elongate, and club shaped. It has two upward-pointing siphons at the top. The tunic is thick and often covered with barnacles, small mussels, and other invertebrates.

Habitat: Found in quiet waters on rocks and pilings, subtidally to 80' (24m).

Range: Massachusetts to Connecticut.

Comments: Originally from Asia, the Club Tunicate was introduced to California and is now found all over southern New England. It was probably brought here on the hulls of ships.

ORANGE SHEATH TUNICATE *Botrylloides violaceus*

Identification: This colonial tunicate forms a thin, soft, fleshy crust. The zooids are arranged in twisting rows. Color—variable, orange, yellow, and reddish. Size: height, 1/8" (3mm); width of colony, 3" (75mm).

Habitat: Found on the hard substrate in bays and protected areas, from the low-tide line to shallow water.

Range: The entire Atlantic Coast.

Comments: This tunicate reproduces by budding, which occurs in the lateral regions of the body. It is preyed upon by gastropods and nudibranchs.

APPENDICULARIAN *Oikopleura labradoriensis*

Identification: This abundant planktonic tunicate has an oval body and a pointed or rounded tail. It surrounds itself with a transparent jelly-like house. Color: house—transparent, body—whitish. Size: body, to 3/8" (9mm); house, 3/4" (18mm).

Habitat: Coastal waters.

Range: Arctic to Delaware; principally found in the northern portion of its range, but can be seen in the southern part of its range during winter and spring.

Comments: The house, an elaborate particle trap, is secreted by epidermal cells. By pumping water through the animal, the house catches rich plankton, which is then consumed. These appendicularians are difficult to see because they are transparent and appear to be just mucus in the water.

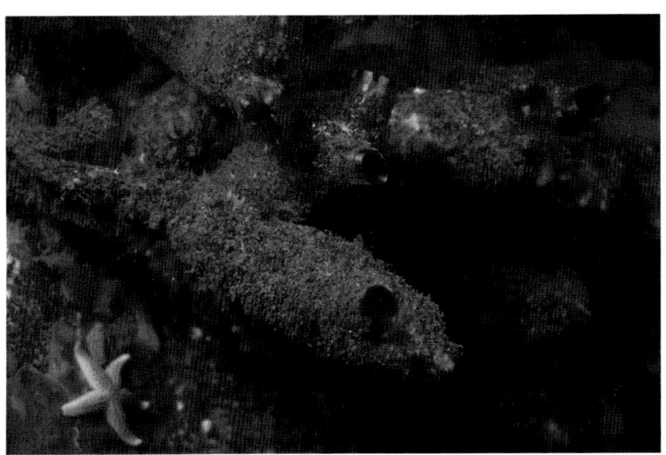

DATE

LOCATION

DATE

LOCATION

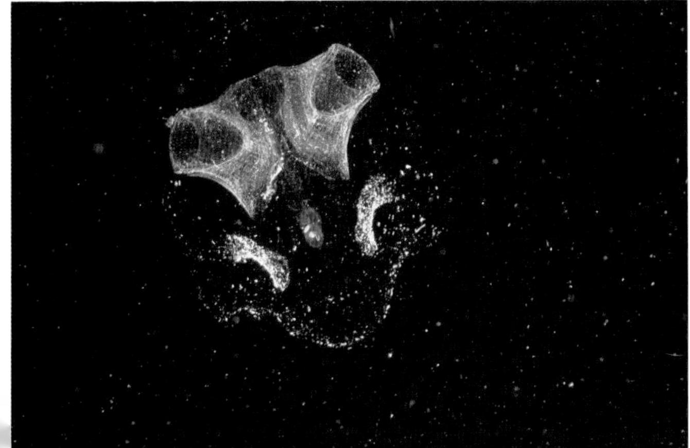

DATE

LOCATION

CHORDATA
(Fish)

Phylum Chordata is a large and varied group of animals, all of which have a segmented spinal column. Every member of this phylum has an internal skeleton and a dorsally located central nervous system. In this book, we will restrict our discussion of marine chordates to fish, which we will divide into two main categories: cartilaginous fish and bony fish.

Fishes of Class Chondrichthyes have a skeleton of cartilage. The best known members are sharks, which live in all the oceans of the world, usually as the top predator in their ecosystem. Rays and skates are also common members. They play a somewhat less obvious, but still integral, part in every ocean ecosystem, either as small predators or scavengers. All representatives of this group have placoid scales, which give the skin the texture of rough sandpaper. They usually have five gill slits but sometimes have as many as seven. The caudal fin is heterocercal, the upper lobe being considerably larger than the lower one.

Reproduction in all cartilaginous fishes is sexual, with internal fertilization. In males, the medial section of each pelvic fin is modified into a copulatory organ called the clasper, which is used in sperm transfer to the female. The mechanism of birth is highly varied within the class. In some species, the young hatch from leathery egg cases laid on the ocean bottom; in other species, the young are born alive. Still other species may hatch from eggs that have been kept in the female's oviduct or nourished by a complex yoke-sac placenta.

In Class Osteichthyes, the skeleton and jaws are formed of true bone instead of cartilage. In all but primitive species, the caudal fin is homocercal, with lobes of about equal size. Both pectoral and pelvic fins are paired. For respiration, there is a single gill opening on each side. If there are scales present, they are generally thin and overlapping. The fins of the bony fish are supported by two basic types of rays—soft or spiny. Soft rays are segmented, a feature that appears as dark lines on the fin. Spines are usually rigid and sharp at the tips. They are not segmented and never branch.

In most bony fishes, sexes are separate and fertilization is external. It occurs when eggs and sperm are concurrently released into the water column and is commonly called spawning. During spawning, some female fish, such as cod, produce as many as 9 million eggs, of which only a small percentage survive. Some bony fish species brood eggs or hatch young in their mouths. In other species, such as lumpfish, the female deposits the eggs, and the male guards them until they are ready to hatch. A very few bony fish species are live bearers; common aquarium fish like guppies fall into this category.

One interesting group of bony fish are the flatfishes (flounders). In the larval stage, one eye migrates to the opposite side of the head, to either the right side or the left side of the fish. Thus, flatfish are classified as right-eyed or left-eyed species. With both eyes on one side, there is now a blind side, which has stronger teeth to compensate for the lack of eyes. The eyed side generally has a better developed pectoral fin and stronger coloration, either cryptic or variable. Most flatfish are chameleon-like and can change color to match the substrate. They can also flip sand on top of their bodies and be remarkably camouflaged as they hide from predators or wait for prey.

Parts of a modern bony fish

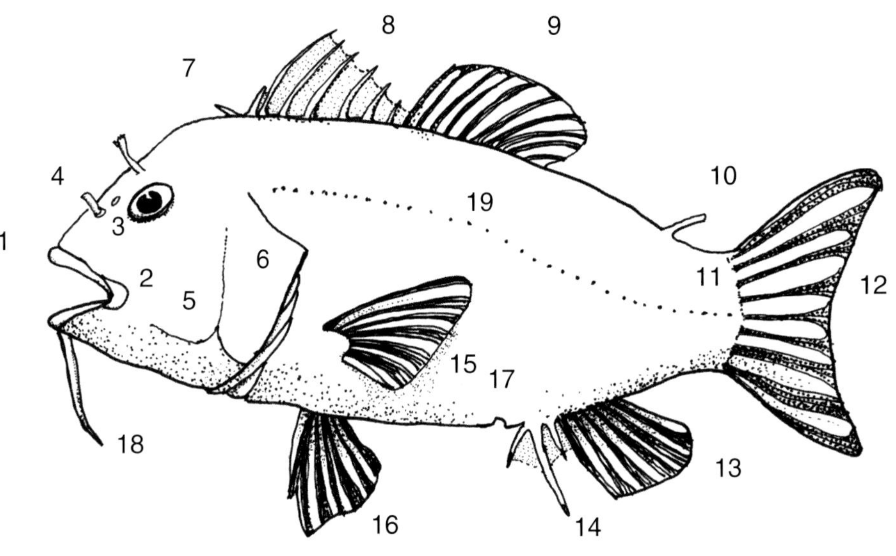

1 premaxilla
2 maxilla
3 nostrils
4 nasal tentacle
5 preoperculum
6 operculum
7 procumbent spine
8 first or spinous dorsal fin
9 second or soft dorsal fin
10 adipose fin
11 caudal peduncle
12 caudal fin or tail
13 anal fin
14 anal spines
15 pectoral fin
16 ventral or pelvic fin
17 anus or vent
18 barbel
19 lateral line

BLUE SHARK *Prionace glauca*

Identification: This graceful, streamlined shark is slender and elongate. It is thickest at the midsection. Snout: long and pointed. Eyes: large. Fins: all slender; pectorals, very long; dorsal, the first is moderate in length, the second is shorter. Color: dark blue on top, changing to lighter blue on the sides and white on the bottom. Size: to 12.5' (3.8m).

Habitat: Pelagic; near the surface in temperate waters, deeper in warm waters.

Range: Nova Scotia to Argentina.

Comments: Travels great distances. One animal tagged in New York was found a year later in Gibraltar. Although these sharks are not considered dangerous to humans, they should be respected. They are stimulated by the scent of blood in the water and have been responsible for many attacks on humans (especially at shipwrecks). The prolific Blue Shark is viviparous and usually produces twenty-five to fifty pups per litter. One recorded litter consisted of 135 pups.

The Blue Shark has very long pectoral fins

SPINY DOGFISH *Squalus acanthias*

Identification: This is a small, slender shark. Head: flattened, with the snout tapering to a point. Fins: the first dorsal fin, which begins at the axis of the pectoral fins, is larger than the second, but the second dorsal has larger spines. Dorsal spines are strong and sharp, but are shorter than the fin. No anal fin. Teeth: small, sharp, similar in both jaws and pointed toward the outer corners of the mouth, forming a continuous cutting edge. Skin: sandpaper-like surface. Color: upper surface is slate gray to brown; sides have white spots; underside is white. Size: to 3.5' (1.1m)

Habitat: Subtidal to 600' (181m).

Range: Labrador to Gulf of Mexico.

Comments: Sport fishermen regard this animal as a bait stealer. Some commercial fishermen sell it as "scallop" or "shark." It is often exported and in Britain, it is usually the fish in "fish and chips." Also known as Dogfish and Grayfish. It is an opportunistic feeder that, nevertheless, prefers small fish.

DATE

LOCATION

DATE

LOCATION

DATE

LOCATION

ATLANTIC TORPEDO *Torpedo nobiliana*

Identification: The body of this electric ray is disc-shaped but blunted forward. The skin is soft, smooth, and without thorns or spines, which helps differentiate it from the skates of this region. The tail is almost as long as the body. Mouth: ventral and small, with tiny teeth. Eyes: small and located far forward. Fins: two dorsal fins located on the forward section of the tail; the first is larger than the second. The caudal fin is not forked. Color: back—brown or gray to black, underside—white. Size: to 6' (1.8m).

Habitat: Found on sand or mud bottoms, near beaches and bays; usually seen in shallow water but has been recorded to a depth of 360' (110m).

Range: Nova Scotia to Florida.

Comments: The Atlantic Torpedo is generally not aggressive. When disturbed, it can produce 220 volts of electricity generated by two organs located on each side of the front part of the body. Feeds on fish, crustaceans, mollusks, and other invertebrates. In years past, the oil from this ray's liver was used for lamps.

Atlantic Torpedo

Atlantic Torpedo buried in the sand

DATE

LOCATION

DATE

LOCATION

DATE

LOCATION

WINTER SKATE *Raja ocellatus*

Identification: The shape of this common skate is a somewhat rounded disc that is wider than it is long and has rounded corners. There are dark spots on the upper surface and four to six irregular rows of spines running from the head to the tail. Head: the tip of the snout is rounded; around the eyes, the head bulges and is covered with sharp thorns. In adult males, the claspers extend halfway down the tail. In adults, the posterior midline is usually free of spines. Fins: the 2 dorsal fins are near each other at the end of the tail. Color: upper surface, brown; usually there is a large, white eye spot with a dark center located near the posterior portion of the pectoral fin. Ventral surface is white. Size: to 43" (1.1m).

Habitat: Gravelly and sandy bottoms, from shallow water to 300' (90m).

Range: Gulf of St. Lawrence to North Carolina.

Comments: This animal's name stems from its coming close to shore in Cape Cod during the winter. It is also known as the Thorny Skate and the Arctic Thorny Skate. Feeds on crustaceans, worms, bivalves, and small fish.

This Winter Skate egg case has just been released by the female

(Bottom, left) After chewing a hole through the side of the egg case, the young emerge

(Bottom, right) The eye of the Winter Skate

DATE

LOCATION

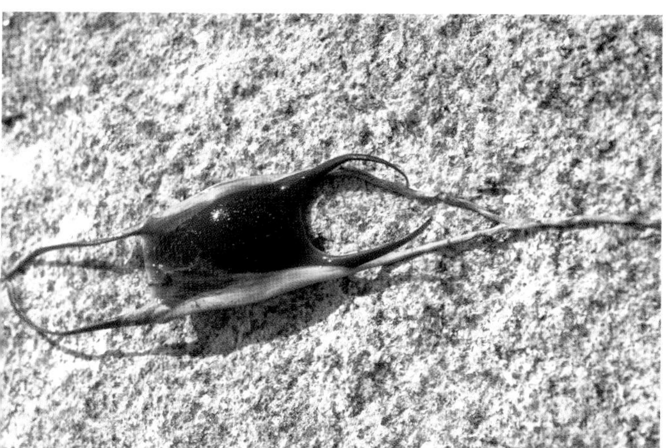

DATE

LOCATION

AMERICAN EEL *Anguilla rostrata*

Identification: The body of this eel is elongate and the anterior cross section is round. Head: snout is pointed, with a large mouth that extends to the eye or just beyond it. The lower jaw extends beyond the upper jaw. Fins: the dorsal fin begins far behind the pectoral fins. These two characteristics are important in distinguishing this species from the conger eel. There is a pair of round nostrils located behind the eyes, which are small and round. As in other eels of the family Anguillidae, there are no ventral fins. As the animal grows, it begins to develop scales, which are so small they are not noticeable. The gill slits are vertical. There is a lateral line. Color: variable—olive brown above, yellowish on the sides; whitish yellow on the bottom. Size: females to 5' (1.5m); males much smaller.

Habitat: Found on muddy bottoms in bays, still waters, and brackish estuaries. It is more active at night when feeding on crustaceans and small fish. In winter it is buried in the mud in lakes or rivers.

Range: Greenland to Gulf of Mexico.

Comments: The eels of this family are catadromous. They migrate from their birthplace (in fresh water) to the sea to spawn and presumably die. During its life, the American Eel may inhabit more than one body of water, even crossing wet, grassy fields to get to lakes and ponds. Edible.

ATLANTIC MENHADEN *Brevoortia tyrannus*

Identification: The body is elongate, compressed laterally, full bellied, and tapered at both ends. The rear edges of the scales are almost vertical and have long, comb-like teeth. Head: very large and scaleless. Mouth: oblique, large, and toothless. The maxillary (lower jaw) extends to or beyond the eye. Fins: dorsal, moderate in size, begins behind the ventral fin; caudal, dark and deeply forked; other fins, yellowish. Color: back—bluish, greenish, and brownish; sides—silvery; dark spot behind gill cover, followed by many irregular dark spots. Size: to 14" (35cm).

Habitat: Found at or near the surface, subtidally to the Continental Shelf.

Range: Nova Scotia to Florida.

Comments: The oily Menhaden is one of the most important commercial fish of the U.S. Atlantic coast. It is not used for human consumption but for fish meal, fertilizers, and oil. Also known as Pogy, Mossbunker, and Fatback. Preyed upon by tuna, bluefish, striped bass, sharks, whales, and sea birds. Feeds on microscopic organisms.

ATLANTIC HERRING *Culpea harengus*

Identification: The shape of this herring is elongated and compressed laterally. Head: small and pointed, with a large mouth and a projecting lower jaw. Teeth: none on the upper jaw, small on the lower. Fins: pectorals, low on sides; dorsal, in the middle of the body; caudal, forked. Color: upper surface—greenish blue, sides and belly—silvery. Size: to 18" (45cm).

Habitat: Along the coast in shallow water especially in bays and lagoons.

Range: Labrador to Cape Hatteras.

Comments: Swims in large schools and feeds on plankton. Spawns in spring, summer, or fall depending on location. Two- to three-year-old herring are known as sardines when canned.

DATE

LOCATION

DATE

LOCATION

DATE

LOCATION

GOOSEFISH *Lophius americanus*

Identification: Compressed dorsally, the body is widest at the pectoral fins, then tapers to a narrow caudal peduncle. Head: flattened, rounded, large, and wider than the body. Mouth: very large, opens upward. The lower jaw projects farther than the upper; both have many large teeth. Both the lower jaw and the sides of the body have a fringe of fleshy appendages. Fins: two dorsal, the first is modified into a fleshy tab (an angling device used to attract prey); pectoral, round and arm-like. Color: back—dark brown, underside—tan, pectoral fins are darker at tips. Size: to 4' (1.2m).

Habitat: Found on the bottom, subtidally to 1,200' (364m).

Range: Gulf of St. Lawrence to northern Florida.

Comments: The Goosefish is a voracious predator and can consume an amazing quantity and variety of animals. It feeds on fish, invertebrates, and seabirds. One Goosefish was found with seven wild ducks in its stomach, another with twenty-one flounders! Also known as Monkfish, Anglerfish, All-mouth, and American Angler. The meat at the base of the tail is considered a delicacy.

ATLANTIC COD *Gadus morhua*

Identification: The body of the Atlantic Cod is elongate, heavy, compressed, and tapers to a slender caudal peduncle. Head: large with a blunt snout. Mouth: large with a protruding upper jaw covered by many small teeth. Eyes: large. There is a chin barbel under the lower jaw. A distinct, light-colored lateral line arches over the pectoral fin. Fins: three separate dorsal fins; one caudal fin, slightly notched; two anal fins. Color: variable—greenish, gray, or reddish with reddish brown spots on back and sides; belly, white. Size: to 6' (1.8m).

Habitat: Found on rocky, pebbly, or sandy bottoms along the continental shelf, from 30' (9m) to 600' (457m).

Range: Arctic to Virginia.

Comments: The color of the Atlantic Cod, a bottom dweller, is affected by its surroundings. The fish will be dark if the rocky bottom is dark. *G. morhua* feeds on capelin, herring, sand eels, and crustaceans. Marine mammals prey on cod. The term Scrod originally referred to small Cod and Haddock. Also known as Codfish or Cod. Highly edible and heavily harvested by commercial and sport fishermen.

POLLOCK *Pollachius virens*

Identification: This pollock is fusiform. Head: moderate in size; pointed snout; lower jaw projects and has a small barbel under chin (absent in larger adults). Fins: three dorsal and two anal. Lateral line is light colored and straight. Color: upper surface—dark greenish brown, becoming yellowish to gray on the sides; underside—grayish. Fins are dark green. Size: to 3.5' (1.1m).

Habitat: From surface to 600' (182m).

Range: Labrador to North Carolina.

Comments: The young eat small fish and crustaceans; adult Pollock prey on fish, mainly small cod, sand eels, and herring. The young are found in large schools while the larger adults are more solitary. Also known as Coalfish Boston Bluefish, and Green Cod. Highly edible and an excellent game fish.

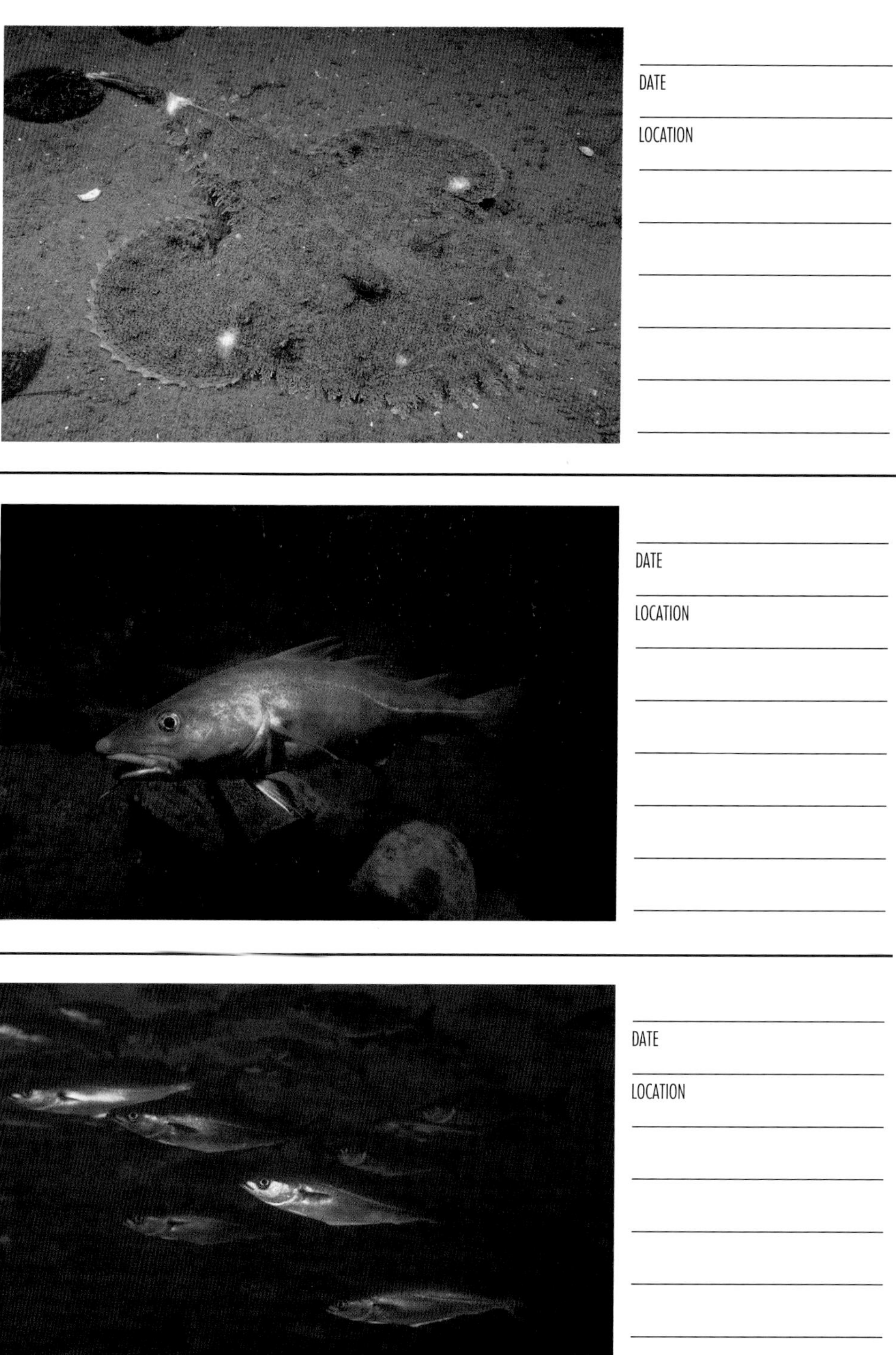

DATE

LOCATION

DATE

LOCATION

DATE

LOCATION

SQUIRREL HAKE *Urophycis chuss*

Identification: The body of this hake is elongate, full around the belly, and laterally compressed behind the anus. Head: small, with a pointed snout. Mouth: large, with a projecting upper jaw. Fins: first dorsal, short with a very long third ray; second dorsal, long and low (reaches caudal peduncle); caudal, rounded; pectoral, longest ray almost reaches the anal fin; anal, short and low (reaches the caudal peduncle). Color: variable—often reddish and mottled, lighter toward the bottom. Size: to 20" (51cm).

Habitat: Found on sand or mud bottoms, subtidal to 3,000' (909m).

Range: Labrador to North Carolina.

Comments: This valuable fish is also known as the Red Hake. It is equipped with sensitive chemoreceptors on its chin barbel, its pelvic fins, and the long ray on its dorsal fin. These help the hake feed at night by sensing its food.

Similar species: White Hake, *U. tenuis,* closely resembles the Squirrel Hake. The upper jaw (maxillary bone) reaches as far as the rear edge of the pupil in the Squirrel Hake, but in the White Hake the upper jaw reaches back as far as the rear of the eye itself.

STRIPED BASS *Morone saxatilis*

Identification: The Striped Bass has an elongated body that is compressed laterally. Head: large and triangular. Mouth: large, with a projecting lower jaw. Snout: long. Eyes: large. Fins: first dorsal, nine spines (sometimes seven to twelve); second dorsal, one spine and twelve branched rays (sometimes eight to fourteen); caudal, forked; pelvic, small, heavy with spines; pectorals, twenty-eight to thirty-seven branched, somewhat pointed rays. Lateral line: straight. Color: dark olive green, varying to blackish and/or bluish above, paling on the sides to white or silver on the belly; sides have seven to eight dark horizontal stripes. Stripes above the lateral line are longer than those below it; the last stripe ends before the anal fin; no stripes on the head. Size: To 6' (1.8m) and 125 pounds (57 kg).

Habitat: Coastal, seldom more than a few miles from shore. Less commonly found in rivers; some are landlocked in freshwater lakes.

Range: St. Lawrence River to northern Florida; in Gulf of Mexico from western Florida to Louisiana.

Comments: Highly prized as a game fish and food fish, the Striped Bass is a voracious, opportunistic feeder. It eats varied small fish, crabs, small lobster, and squid.

NORTHERN PIPEFISH *Syngnathus fuscus*

Identification: This small fish is elongate and slender. The body is hexagonal in cross section anterior to the anus, but posterior to that it is four sided. *S. fuscus* has an armor of bony plates that are connected in rings. There are eighteen to twenty-one plates before the anus and thirty-four to thirty-nine behind. Head: short, thin, and tapering Snout: tubular. Mouth: toothless and small. Eyes: located high on the head, they rotate independently. Fins: dorsal five times longer than it is high; caudal, rounded; ventral, none. Color: upper surface—mottled greenish to brown lower parts of sides have white dots; ventral surface—yellowish. Color: can change according to location. Size: to 12" (30cm).

Habitat: Found in eel grass or seaweed in bays and estuaries.

Range: Newfoundland to Gulf of Mexico.

Comments: Feeds on copepods, amphipods, and minute organisms. Has few enemies. The male incubates the egg on his body.

DATE

LOCATION

DATE

LOCATION

DATE

LOCATION

BLACK SEA BASS *Centropristis striata*

Identification: This moderately full-bodied bass has a flat head and a high back. Snout: somewhat pointed. Mouth: large. Eyes: high on the head. Fins: dorsal, continuous (front half is spiny, rear is soft rayed); anal, rounded; caudal, rounded with white upper and lower edges. In larger specimens, the upper ray of the caudal fin is longer. Color: dark gray to black to brown, mottled. White spots on center of scales create light stripes. Males tend to be blue black. Size: to 24" (61cm).

Habitat: Found on rocky bottoms, from the shore line to 420' (127m).

Range: Maine to Florida.

Comments: Feeds on lobsters, crabs, shrimp, small fish, and squid. Highly edible.

TAUTOG *Tautoga onitis*

Identification: The body of the Tautog is oblong, stout, and compressed laterally. Head, steep in profile, with a blunt snout. Mouth: small with thick lips (located low on the head). Teeth: those in front are heavy and larger; rear teeth are flat, rounded, and used for crushing. Eyes: moderate size. Fins: dorsal, long with sixteen to seventeen spines; caudal, wide and squared; anal fin, one. Color: blackish with mottled sides. Size: to 3' (91 cm).

Habitat: Found on rocky shores, along breakwaters and wrecks, intertidally to 60' (18m).

Range: Nova Scotia to South Carolina.

Comments: The Tautog uses its powerful jaws and strong teeth to feed on crustaceans, mussels, and other mollusks. It is considered a good game fish and is highly edible. Also known as Blackfish.

CUNNER *Tautogolabrus adspersus*

Identification: The body is oblong and compressed laterally; the caudal peduncle is thick. Head: pointed. Mouth: terminal and small, with a front row of strong, conical teeth. Fins: dorsal, long; caudal, thick and somewhat rounded. The lateral line is complete and curves downward at the posterior. Color: variable—above, mottled with greenish, reddish, bluish, and brownish; underneath, whitish or bluish. Juveniles have a black spot at the front of the dorsal fin. Size: to 15" (38cm).

Habitat: Found in shallow water, close to shore, around pilings, seawalls, and rocky areas, to 425' (129m).

Range: Newfoundland to Chesapeake Bay.

Comments: This omnivorous fish feeds on mollusks, sea urchins, crustaceans, worms, and crabs. Fishermen consider it a pest and bait-stealer. Feeding slows down during the winter months. Also known as Bergall and Sea Perch.

DATE

LOCATION

DATE

LOCATION

DATE

LOCATION

ARCTIC SHANNY *Stichaeus punctatus*

Identification: The body is elongate and somewhat compressed laterally. Head: pointed. Mouth: small and terminal, with the lower jaw projecting farther than the upper. Eyes: moderate in size with a small space between them. Fins: dorsal, long with five dark marks; caudal, round and separate from dorsal and anal fins; pelvic, small. Lateral line: single and incomplete. Color: brownish to red, whitish underneath; six to seven dark bars on lower part of head; mottled on sides; Size: to 9" (22 cm).

Habitat: Found on rocky bottoms, subtidally to 180' (54m).

Range: Arctic to Maine.

Comments: Feeds on small amphipods and other crustaceans. Major predators are cod, halibut, and the black guillemot, a sea bird. Also known as the Spotted Snakeblenny.

Arctic Shanny color variation

RADIATED SHANNY *Ulvaria subbifurcata*

Identification: The body is stout, elongate, and eel-like. Head: rounded. Mouth: terminal, with both jaws of equal length. Teeth: small. Eyes: large. Fins: dorsal, long (joins the rounded caudal fin by means of a membrane); has a large oval spot toward the anterior. Anal, long (does not reach the caudal fin). Lateral line: two are present. Color: brown to yellowish, becoming more yellow below. Size: to 7" (16 cm).

Habitat: Found near seaweeds and on rocky bottoms, subtidally to 180' (54m).

Range: Newfoundland to southern Massachusetts.

Comments: Feeds nocturnally on crustaceans and worms. The predators of the Radiated Shanny are benthic diurnal (daytime) feeders; that causes it to spend much of its time hiding until the safety of night. Also known as the Shanny.

DATE

LOCATION

DATE

LOCATION

DATE

LOCATION

ROCK GUNNEL *Pholis gunnellus*

Identification: The body is elongate and laterally compressed, tapering to the caudal peduncle. A dark bar runs upward from the eye to the dorsal fin; below the eye, it curves downward to just behind the mouth. Head: small, with a blunt snout. Mouth, terminal and oblique. Fins: dorsal, short, extending from behind the head to the caudal fin; anal, short extending from the anus to the caudal fin. Lateral line, absent. There are ten to fourteen equally spaced black spots that are outlined with pale edges. Color: variable—yellowish to reddish to greenish. Size: 1' (30cm).

Habitat: Rocky and algae-covered bottoms, from tide pools to 600' (182m).

Range: Labrador to Delaware Bay.

Comments: Rock Gunnels spawn in the winter, and parents guard the eggs. Preyed upon by cod, pollock and, in shallow water, sea birds. Feeds on worms and crustaceans. Also known as Tansy, Butterfish, and Rock Eel.

Similar species: Banded Gunnel, *P. fasciata.*

Rock Gunnel color variation

A second Rock Gunnel color variation

DATE

LOCATION

DATE

LOCATION

DATE

LOCATION

ATLANTIC WOLFFISH *Anarhichas lupus*

Identification: The body is stout behind the head then tapers to a slender caudal peduncle. Head: large, with a blunt snout. Mouth: terminal and large, with large canine teeth. Fins: dorsal, long (extending to the caudal peduncle); caudal, small and rounded; anal, half of the body length; pectorals, rounded. Color: variable—gray, slate blue, or brownish, with irregular markings on sides. Size: 5' (1.5m).

Habitat: Found on rocky bottoms, from 6' (1.8m) to 1,000' (303m).

Range: Greenland to Cape Cod.

Comments: The Atlantic Wolffish is often seen hiding in crevices along rock walls and slopes. It feeds on small fish and a wide variety of invertebrates. Also known as Catfish, Striped Wolffish, and Ocean Wolffish. Edible.

(Right) The Atlantic Wolffish is often seen in a crevice in the rocks

---

OCEAN POUT *Macrozoarces americanus*

Identification: The body is elongate, stout, and eel-like, tapering to the rear. Head: broad. Snout: blunt. Mouth: terminal and large; the upper jaw projects farther than the lower. Teeth: two series of strong teeth in the front of the jaws. Fins: dorsal, long (almost the length of the back); anal, long; pectoral, rounded. Color: variable—gray, yellowish, and reddish brown; the mottled dorsal is darker. Size: to 3.5' (1.1m).

Habitat: Found on all bottoms but more often on hard ground, intertidally to 595' (183m).

Range: Gulf of St. Lawrence to Delaware.

Comments: Feeds on most invertebrates and small fish. Also known as Muttonfish, Congo Eel, and Eelpout.

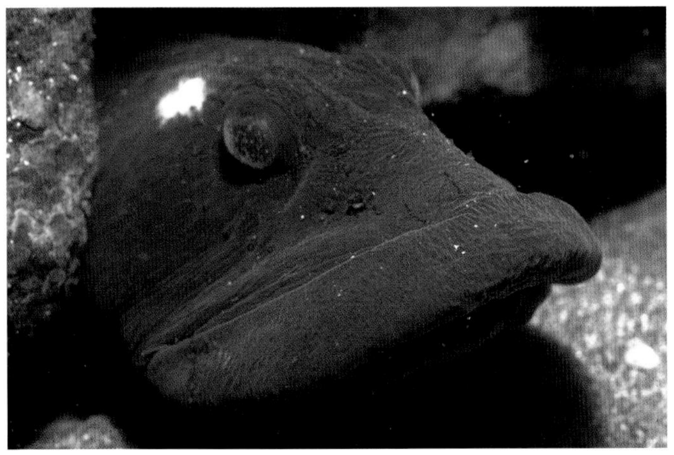

(Left) The mouth of the Ocean Pout

(Bottom, right) Ocean Pout

DATE

LOCATION

DATE

LOCATION

DATE

LOCATION

ROSE FISH *Sebastes fasciatus*

Identification: The body of the Rose Fish is compressed laterally and somewhat oval shaped; it tapers to the caudal peduncle. Head: sloping; the lower jaw juts out and features a bony protuberance that fits into a notch in the upper jaw. The sides of the head have spines. Eyes: dark. Fins: dorsal, long, running from behind the head to the caudal peduncle; anal, shorter than the soft portion of the dorsal; pectoral, large. Color: reddish or orange. Size: to 20" (51cm).

Habitat: Found on or near rocky bottoms, to 270' (82m).

Range: Gulf of St. Lawrence to New Jersey.

Comments: This slow-growing species feeds on small fish, crustaceans, small mollusks, and other invertebrates. It is preyed upon by many large fish.

NORTHERN SEA ROBIN *Prionotus carolinus*

Identification: The body is elongate; wide in the front, it tapers to the tail. Head: large, encased in bony plates; snout, depressed dorsally. Fins: pectoral, wing-like; three lower rays are separate from the main fins and are modified so that they appear as walking legs. Color: above—reddish brown to gray, mottled with dark spots; below—whitish to light yellow; there is a black spot between the fourth and sixth dorsal spines. Size: to 16" (40cm).

Habitat: Found on sandy or hard bottoms, from 25' to 240' (8m to 73m).

Range: Nova Scotia to Florida.

Comments: This sea robin partially buries itself in the sand for defense and to surprise its prey. It feeds on small animals by using its "walking legs" to stir up the bottom.

(Middle and bottom, left) The pectoral fins of the Northern Sea Robin are wing-like

(Bottom, right) The Northern Sea Robin lies buried in the sand as it waits for prey

DATE

LOCATION

DATE

LOCATION

SEA RAVEN *Hemitripterus americanus*

Identification: The body is prickly and elongate, with a stout anterior tapering to a moderate caudal peduncle. Head: large, with many skin flaps. Mouth: large, with several fleshy tabs on lower jaw. Fins: first dorsal, ragged in appearance; second dorsal, separated from the first by a short space; caudal, large and rounded. Lateral line, moderately high on the body. Color: variable—red, yellow, and reddish brown. Size: to 25" (64 mm).

Habitat: Found on rocky bottoms, from 6' (2m) to 300' (91m).

Range: Labrador to Chesapeake Bay.

Comments: The Sea Raven, well disguised, waits for small fish to approach before it lunges forward to attack. It feeds on bottom-living invertebrates and small fishes. When Sea Ravens are removed from the water, they sometimes inflate their bellies with air and can not submerge themselves upon reentering the water. Also known as Atlantic Sea Raven, Puff-belly, Sea Hen, and Scratch-belly.

The Sea Raven has a large mouth that helps it swallow its victims

(Left) Sea Raven color variation.

(Bottom, right) Another Sea Raven color variation

DATE

LOCATION

DATE

LOCATION

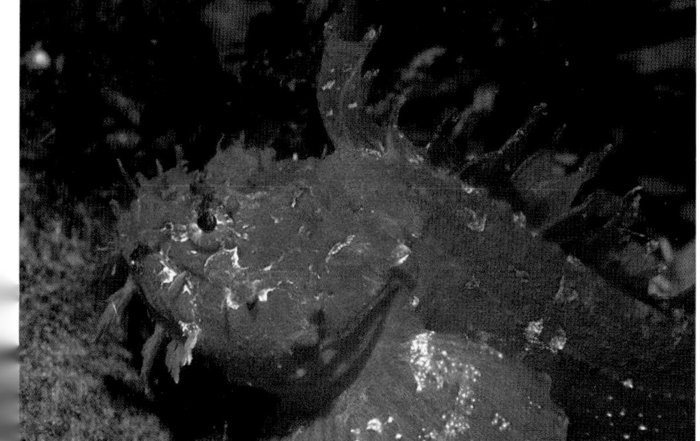

DATE

LOCATION

SHORTHORN SCULPIN *Myoxocephalus scorpius*

Identification: The elongated body tapers to the caudal peduncle. Head: large and flat, with one short spine before the eyes, two behind the eyes (in the center of the head), and five to seven short, blunt, triangular spines on each side of the cheeks (between the snout and gill opening). Snout: tapers to the large mouth. Eyes: large and placed high on the sides of the head. Fins: first dorsal, seven to twelve spines; second dorsal, twelve to twenty soft rays; caudal, moderate and rounded; pelvic, one spine and three soft rays. The lateral line is complete. Color: variable—reddish, dark green, or brown above, with mottling or bars; whitish or yellowish on underside (males have large blotches underneath). Size: to 20" (50cm).

Habitat: Found on rocky bottoms, subtidally to 360' (110m).

Range: Arctic to New York.

Comments: The blotches on the underside of males are more pronounced during the mating period. The Shorthorn Sculpin is a voracious feeder, consuming a wide variety of mollusks, crustaceans, squid, and small fish.

Shorthorn Sculpin color variation

A second color variation in the Shorthorn Sculpin

DATE

LOCATION

DATE

LOCATION

DATE

LOCATION

GRUBBY *Myoxocephalus aenaeus*

Identification: The body is moderately elongated, tapering to a somewhat narrow caudal peduncle. Head: broad, with smooth skin and a ridge on top; one or two spines over each eye; a pair of short spines over each nostril; three short spines on preopercle (the lowest one is pointed), and three spines on the opercle. Mouth: terminal, with a protruding upper jaw. Eyes: large, high on head. Fins: first dorsal, eight to ten spines; second dorsal, eleven to fourteen soft rays; caudal, rounded; pelvic, one spine, three soft rays; pectorals, large and wide; anal, ten or eleven soft rays. The lateral line is prominent and high. Color: varies with the bottom—sides, light to dark gray with dark shadings; belly, light gray to white; fins, broken bars. Size: to 6" (15cm).

Habitat: Coastal, found on sand, gravel, mud, and in eel grass.

Range: Gulf of St. Lawrence to New Jersey.

Comments: Feeds on small crabs, worms, urchins, tunicates, and the juveniles of many fish species. It is preyed upon by larger fish such as cod. Also known as Little Sculpin.

LONGHORN SCULPIN *Myoxocephalus octodecimspinosus*

Identification: The elongated body is not as stout as that of the Shorthorn Sculpin at the first dorsal fin; it tapers to the caudal peduncle. Head: large and flat with one pair of short, nasal spines; there is an additional pair of spines above and behind the eyes and a pair farther behind the eyes, on top of the head. There are three cheek spines—the upper one is sharp, raked at the tip, and four times as long as the one below it; the lower (third) spine turns downward. Mouth: large. Snout: tapers to mouth. Eyes: large, high on the sides of the head. The lateral line has a series of calcified plates. Color: above, variable—olive, gray, and yellowish; below, white. Size: to 18" (46cm).

Habitat: Found on rocky bottoms close to shore, subtidally to 400' (121m).

Range: Gulf of St. Lawrence to Virginia.

Comments: The Longhorn Sculpin, like the Shorthorn, is a voracious feeder, consuming a wide variety of mollusks, crustaceans, squid, and small fish. Also known as the Long-spine Sculpin, Hacklehead, Bullhead, and Gray Sculpin.

ALLIGATORFISH *Aspidophoroides monopterygius*

Identification: The body is elongate, slender, and smooth. In a cross section, anterior is octagonal and posterior is hexagonal. Entire head and body covered with bony plates. Head: small, somewhat depressed, and no barbells. Mouth: terminal, small. Fins: dorsal, 1st absent, second 5-6 soft rays; caudal, somewhat large, rounded; anal 4-6 soft rays; pelvics, small; pectorals, long, and fan-like. Color: dark brown above and lighter below. Two dark bands in front of the dorsal fin. Size: to 7" (18cm).

Habitat: Found in sand or muddy bottoms, 6' to 60' (18-192m).

Range: West Greenland to Cape Cod and occasionally New Jersey.

Comments: It is preyed upon by cod and haddock.

DATE

LOCATION

DATE

LOCATION

DATE

LOCATION

LUMPFISH *Cyclopterus lumpus*

Identification: The body of the Lumpfish is thick and stout, with a hump on the top. Along the mid-back, there is a row of noticeable tubercles, and there are three other, similar rows along each side. Head: short and blunt. Mouth: small and terminal. Eyes: moderate in size. Fins: dorsal, two; caudal, moderate, somewhat rounded; pelvic, modified to six pairs of fleshy knobs that are surrounded by a circular tab of skin. This forms an adhesive disc that is used as a suction cup to hold the fish on hard substrate. Color: variable—often matches the surroundings; above, red, gray, bluish, and brownish; below, yellowish or white, except in breeding males, which is red. Size: to 2' (61cm).

Habitat: Found on rocky bottoms, from 6' (2m) to 1,100' (333m).

Range: Greenland to New Jersey.

Comments: The male uses the "suction cup" to hold its position as it guards the eggs deposited by the female. He keeps these eggs, which are sold as caviar, aerated and clean by blowing water on them. The Lumpfish feeds on a wide variety of invertebrates and small fish. It is preyed upon by seals, sperm whales, and the Greenland Shark. Juvenile Lumpfish are often found clinging to kelp and other seaweed. Also known as Henfish, Lump, and Lumpsucker.

Lumpfish guarding eggs

(Left) The Lumpfish has a short, blunt head

(Right) A male Lumpfish aerates eggs

DATE

LOCATION

DATE

LOCATION

DATE

LOCATION

ATLANTIC SPINY LUMPSUCKER *Eumicrotremus spinosus*

Identification: The body is stout and short, broadest before the first dorsal fin, tapering to the slender caudal peduncle, and covered with tubercles. Head: large. Snout: blunt and round. Mouth: small with big lips. Fins: dorsal, two; caudal, small and somewhat round; pelvic, modified to form an adhesive disc (see Lumpfish entry, p. 248). Color: yellow, orange, greenish, brownish, and reddish brown. Size: to 5" (13 cm).

Habitat: Found on rocky or gravelly bottoms, subtidally to 275' (82m).

Range: Arctic to Maine.

Comments: With large, irregular lumps all over its body, the Atlantic Spiny Lumpsucker, is easily distinguished from a juvenile Lumpfish. It is preyed upon by cod, other large fish, and thick-billed murres.

Atlantic Spiny Lumpsucker color variation

NORTHERN PUFFER *Sphoeroides maculatus*

Identification: The moderately slender body is round at the head and begins to taper at the gills. It is narrow at the caudal peduncle. Mouth: small, located at tip of the snout. Teeth: absent (bones of upper and lower jaws provide cutting edges). Eyes: oval, located high on head. The puffer's skin has no scales, but there are small stiff prickles on the underside between the head and anus. Additional prickles cover the belly and sides, from the anus to the tail; these are sharp, they point toward the tail, and—when the fish inflates itself—they become erect. The prickles on the puffer's back are blunt and erect. Fins: dorsal and anal, short, lacking spines, located near the caudal peduncle; ventral, none. Color: above—dark olive to dark gray; sides—yellowish to orange with six to eight dark blotchy bands; belly—white. Size: to 14" (35cm). Females larger than males.

Habitat: Found on sand or mud, subtidally to 180' (55m); often near estuaries, rarely beyond one to two miles (1.6 to 3.2km) from shore.

Range: Newfoundland to Florida.

Comments: When disturbed, this puffer can inflate its belly with air or water and assume the shape of a balloon.

DATE

LOCATION

DATE

LOCATION

DATE

LOCATION

SUMMER FLOUNDER *Paralichthys dentatus*

Identification: This left-eyed flounder is more ovate than round. There are many ocelli on the the upper surface: Five large ones are always present—one in the middle on the lateral line; two near the base of the dorsal fin; two directly below those (near the base of anal fin). Fins: ventral, both alike but separated from the long anal fin. Mouth: large. Color: varies to match surroundings—upper, gray or brown; underneath, white. Size: to 3' (.9m), but usually 22" (55cm).

Habitat: On sandy or muddy bottoms, from shore to 480' (146m). *P. dentatus* stays in the deeper part of this range in the winter. In summer, the smaller fish come closer to shore, while the larger ones stay in depths of 40' to 60' (12m to 18m).

Range: Maine to Florida.

Comments: This flounder's color changes are more variable than those of most flatfish in this region. It feeds on small fish, mollusks, squid, and shrimp. It has been seen pursuing small schools of minnows up to the surface. Also known as Fluke, it is much sought after by anglers and makes excellent table fare.

FOURSPOT FLOUNDER *Paralichthys oblongus*

Identification: This species is similar to the Summer Flounder but smaller. The gray, mottled upper side has four large oblong dark ocelli that are outlined in light pink. Size: to 16" (41cm).

Habitat: In the northern part of the range, it is found in bays and sounds; in the southern part of the range, it may be seen to 900' (275m).

Range: Georges Bank to Florida.

Comments: *P. oblongus* spawns in the late spring and early summer; the eggs are buoyant. Its diet is similar to that of the Summer Flounder.

WINDOWPANE FLOUNDER *Scophthalmus aquosus*

Identification: This left-eyed flounder is very thin and almost round, with many dark spots on the body and fins. The lateral line is greatly arched at its forward end. Mouth: large, with projecting lower jaw. Fins: caudal, round; first dorsal (closest to the head), rays are branched toward the tip, an identifying feature of this species. Color: brownish, olive, and grayish. Size: to 18" (45cm).

Habitat: Found on sandy bottoms, from shore to 150' (46m).

Range: Gulf of St Lawrence to Florida.

Comments: Of little commercial value, this flatfish is so thin that when held up to sunlight, its body is translucent. It feeds on shrimp, worms, crabs, tunicates, other invertebrates, and small fish. *S. aquosus* spawns in late spring and early summer.

DATE

LOCATION

DATE

LOCATION

DATE

LOCATION

WINTER FLOUNDER *Pleuronectes americanus*

Identification: This flounder is ovate and strongly compressed laterally. Head: of moderate size. Mouth: small, terminates in front of the eye; lower jaw projects somewhat. Eyes: moderate, both on the right side. Fins: dorsal, soft rayed; caudal, rounded. The lateral line is almost straight. Color: eyed side, reddish brown, dark brown, greenish, and grayish; patterns are changeable—may be blotched, mottled, or spotted; blind side, white. Size: to 25" (64 cm).

Habitat: Found on sandy or hard bottoms, subtidally to 475' (143m).

Range: Labrador to Georgia.

Comments: The Winter Flounder has the ability to change its color to match the surroundings. In experiments, this species was able to match the checkerboard bottom on which it was placed. It feeds on worms, crustaceans, mollusks, and other animals that live on the bottom. In shallow water, juveniles are preyed upon by herons and cormorants. Also known as Lemon Sole, Blackback flounder, Sole, and Dab.

The Winter Flounder is a right-eyed flatfish. Compare the orientation of its mouth with that of the Summer Flounder, a left-eyed species.

(Left) Winter Flounder buried in the sand

(Right) The Winter Flounder is capable of blending in with the substrate

DATE

LOCATION

DATE

LOCATION

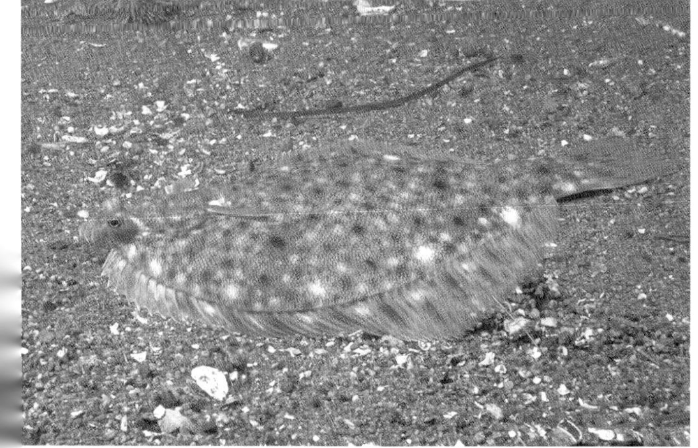

DATE

LOCATION

GLOSSARY

A

Abdomen The posterior part of a body that is divided into distinct regions.

Aboral Situated opposite to or away from the mouth.

Acontia In some sea anemones, the threadlike material protruded through small pores; armed with nematocyst cells, the asconti are used to protect the anemone when it is severely disturbed.

Adductor muscle In bivalve mollusks, a large muscle that pulls the valves of the shell together.

Anadromous Pertaining to marine fish that enter fresh water to spawn.

Anal fin The single fin located just to the rear of the anus.

Antenna (plural: antennae) In arthropods, one of a pair of joined sensory appendages on the head (crustaceans have two pairs of antennae; insects have one pair).

Anterior At or near the front end of the body.

Anus The exit end of the alimentary canal, opposite the mouth.

Aperture The opening or entrance of the shell.

Apex The top of the spire of a snail's shell.

Appendicularian A class of planktonic tunicates.

Aristotle's lantern A group of five teeth and some accessory structures associated with the mouths of sand dollars and sea urchins; used for breaking up food.

Asexual reproduction Reproduction not involving sex cells.

Asymmetrical Without geometric balance.

Atrial siphon In a tunicate, the tube from which water is expelled.

Axial rib In gastropods, a rib running from spire to base.

B

Barbel The fleshy, whisker-like projection seen in the lower part of the head of fish such as sea ravens.

Beak The initial part of a bivalve (see umbo).

Bilateral symmetry A type of geometric balance in which the body can be divided down the midline into two equal halves.

Binary Fission A type of asexual reproduction in which the organism divides itself into two fairly equal parts.

Blade The "leaf" in leafy forms of algae.

Blastula A stage that terminates the cleavage of cells in many animal eggs; usuallya hollow sphere of cells.

Blotch An area of color with an irregular outline.

Blue-green Algae Zone An area high on the rocky coast, farthest from the water yet regularly wet by high tide.

Body whorl In gastropods, the final and usually largest coil or spiral.

Brackish Consisting of a mixture of salt and fresh water.

Branchial siphon In tunicates, the tube through which water enters.

Brood sac A part of the adult's body that protects the eggs.

Brooder An animal that protects its eggs until they hatch.

Bryozoan A colonial animal that lives in a hard protective case that features an opening through which tentacles extend. These tentacles are ciliated and surround the mouth.

Budding Asexual reproduction in which a small portion of the original animal splits off and subsequently develops into a whole, new individual.

Byssus In bivalve mollusks, organic material (protein) usually in the form of threads, used for attachment. It is formed by a gland at the base of the foot.

C

Calcareous Composed of calcium carbonate.

Canopy A species of plant that can grow high enough in the intertidal zone to shade most plants below.

Carapace In crustaceans, a hard portion of the exoskeleton that covers the head and thorax.

Cartilage Translucent tissue that makes up most of the skeleton of very young fishes; it usually converts to bone as the animal grows. In sharks and rays, it persists in the adult.

Carrageenin (or carragheen) The gelatin-like material obtained from Chondrus and other red algae; used commercially as a thickener.

Catadromous Pertaining to species that pass from fresh water to salt water for reproductive reasons. Example: the American Eel.

Caudal fin Tail fin.

Caudal peduncle The tapered part of a fish's body just before the caudal fin.

Cephalic Pertaining to or near the head.

Cephalothorax In arthropods, the forward section of the body, consisting of a head and one or more thoracic segments.

Cerata In nudibranchs, the fleshy projections of the upper surface, generally with branches of the digestive tract connected to them.

Chela In arthropods, the end of a limb that forms a claw.

Chelifores In sea spiders, the first pair of appendages.

Chelipeds In arthropods, the principal claw-bearing appendages.

Chitin In arthropods, the substance (protein) of the skin or shell.

Chitinous Made of chitin, above.

Choanocyte In sponges, a flagellated cell with a collar that creates a current which draws water into the animal.

Chondrophore In bivalves, the spoon-like tooth under the beak of the left valve.

Chromatophore The pigment cell in the skin of fish, octopuses, and squid. Its color crystals can be made to expand or contract, thus changing the animal's apparent color.

Cilia (singular: cilium) Microscopic hairlike projections of cells (similar to flagella); important in creating water currents for locomotion and/or feeding.

Ciliary plate In ctenophores, the fused plates of cilia used for locomotion.

Cirrus (plural: cirri) A soft, generally finger or tentacle-like appendage.

Clasper(s) The elongated part of a male shark, ray, or skate's pelvic fin; used in copulation.

Cnidocyte In Cnidarians, a cell that contains a nematocyst, or stinging capsule.

Colloblasts Sticky cells on the tentacles of ctenophores; used in capturing food.

Columella In gastropods, the pillar around which the whorls, or spirals, form.

Commensalism An association between two species in which one lives on, in, or with the other, receiving some benefit from the relationship, but neither harming nor benefiting its host.

Contractile Able to contract, such as the tentacles of cnidarians.

Convex Curved or rounded like the exterior of a sphere.

Cryptic Hidden or concealing.

Ctenophore A jelly-like animal (phylum Ctenophora) that generally has eight rows of ciliary plates. It lacks the stinging cells of true jellyfish.

D

Detritus Fine organic matter derived from the disintegration of animals or plants.

Diatoms A group of one-celled plants characterized by cell walls that contain silica. Part of the phytoplankton.

Dichotomous In plants, characterized by the division of a branch into two equal parts.

Dioecious Having male sex organs in one individual and female in another.

Dorsal fin The fin lying along the back of a fish.

Dorsal Referring to the upper surface or back of the body.

E

Ecdysis In arthropods, the shedding of the exoskeleton; molting.

Ecto- A prefix referring to something that is external.

Endo- A prefix referring to something that is internal.

Epidermis The outer cellular layer of skin.

Epiphyte A plant that lives on another plant without extracting anything from the relationship other than a place to live.

Errant In Annelid worms, those that are free living and predatory.

Estuary The area where a river or stream meets the sea.

Eversible Able to turn inside out and protrude at the same time; example: the pharynx of some invertebrates.

Exoskeleton An external skeleton, as in crabs, lobsters, and other arthropods.

F

Family In taxonomy, the subdivision of an order.

Flagella (singular: flagellum) Whip-like projections of cells, important in creating water currents to aid in locomotion, and feeding. They are structurally similar to cilia, but the term flagella is used when there is only one such projection or just a few.

Flotsam Material brought up on the beach by high tide.

Foot In mollusks, the organ used for digging and crawling.

Fouling Organisms such as algae or barnacles growing on the surface of manmade objects likes boats and dock pilings.

Frond In alga, a blade or leaf-like structure.

Fugative A plant that is an opportunist, taking advantage of openings in the canopy and colonizings those areas.

Fusiform A long streamlined shape, associated with some fish.

G

Gastrodermis The layer of cells that lines the digestive cavity.

Genus A group of species that have one or more anatomical characteristics in common.

Gills A series of membranes in each side of the head; in fish, they serve as lungs.

Gill ring On the dorsal side of some nudibranchs, a circle of appendages used for respiration.

Girdle The muscular band that surrounds and holds together the valves of a chiton.

Gonads Sex glands—ovaries or testes.

H

Habitat The living environment of an organism.

Herbivorous Feeding on vegetation only.

Hermaphrodite Having both male and female sex organs.

Heterocercal In fish, having an unequally divided caudal fin. The spinal column runs into the much larger, upper lobe.

Hinge The place where the two valves of a bivalve meet.

Holdfast The base of an alga (seaweed); what the plant uses to attach itself to the substrate.

Homocercal In fish, having an equally divided caudal fin. The spinal column ends at the base of the tail.

Host An organism that provides a home for another species in or on itself.

House In appendicularians, the bubble-like mucus mass that is secreted by the animal, which is then surrounded by it.

Hydranth The feeding part of a hydroid colony, equipped with a mouth and tentacles.

Hydrotheca In hydroids, a covering that surrounds and protects the hydranth.

I

Intertidal The area between the high-tide line and the low-tide line.

Invertebrates Animals that lack a spinal column.

J

Juvenile (noun) A fish during its early stages.

L

Labial furrows Grooves at the corners of the mouth of some sharks and rays.

Larva (plural: larvae) A developmental stage, differing from an embryo in that it is able to secure its own nourishment. Almost all larvae differ markedly from the adult in appearance and attain the adult shape by metamorphosis.

Lateral At the side; to one side of the midline.

Lateral line A sensory organ found in fish; consists of a canal running along the side of the body and opening to the outside through a series of pores.

Littoral Of the tidal zone; intertidal.

M

Madreporite In echinoderms, the porous plate through which the internal water-vascular system opens to the exterior. Also called the sieve plate.

Mantle In mollusks, the outer sheet of tissue that encloses the animal's soft structures. It also secretes the shell.

Mandibles In crustaceans, the pair of appendages behind the antennae.

Manubrium In hydromedusae, the long tube on which the mouth is located.

Maxillae (singular: maxilla) The first pair of appendages after the mandibles; mouth parts.

Margin In medusae, the edge of the bell.

Median Pertaining to the midline.

Medusa (plural: medusae) In contrast to the polyp, the free-swimming, jellyfish-like form of the cnidarian.

Membranous frontal wall The membrane that forms the outer or "front" of the encrusting animal, as in bryozoans.

Mesogloea In ctenophores and cnidarians, the middle "jelly," a largely non cellular layer between the cellular layers that line the digestive cavity and cover the outer surface of the body.

Mobile Able to move about freely, not fixed.

Molt In arthropods, to shed the exoskeleton.

Monoecious Having male and female sex organs in a single organism.

Mouth arms In medusae, the tentacle-like appendages that extend down from the sides of the mouth.

Mutualism A type of association between two species that is of mutual benefit to both.

Myofibril A unit of muscle fiber.

N

Nematocyst In cnidarians, a stinging capsule.

Notochord A skeletal rod present at some stage of development in all chordates. In higher vertebrates, it turns into the vertebrae, while in other chordates, it is simply a turgid rod of cells lying immediately beneath and parallel to the nerve cord.

O

Obligate epiphyte A plant that lives in an extremely close relationship with another plant, so that no alternate host or habitat is acceptable.

Ocellus (plural: ocelli) An eyespot; a simple photoreceptor that can distinguish a light source but not form an image.

Octant In jellyfish, one of the eight sections of the umbrella, or bell.

Omnivorous Feeding on both plants and animals.

Operculum In gastropods, the trap door used for closing the shell after the animal withdraws.

Oral disc The flattened upper surface of anemones and polyps. The mouth is at the center, and a ring of tentacles surrounds it.

Oral Relating to the mouth or the end of the body on which the mouth is located.

Osculum (plural: oscula) In sponges, an opening through which water passes *out of* the body.

Ostium (plural: ostia) In sponges, an opening through which water passes *into* the body.

Ovate Oval shaped.

Oxea In sponges, a spicule that is long, thin, and tapered at both ends.

P

Palps In crustaceans, an appendage located near the mouth; generally used for taste or touch.

Pallial line In bivalves, a scar on the inner base of the shell, where the mantle is held fast to the lower part.

Pallial sinus In bivalves, an indentation in the pallial line.

Papilla (plural: papillae) Any small, conical protuberance on the body wall.

Parapodium (plural: parapodia) In polychaete annelids, the fleshy flap of tissue on each side of most segments.

Parasite An organism that lives on or in another organism and obtains nourishment from it.

Paxilla (plural: paxillae) A column-like projection, often topped with spines; found on the skin of sea stars.

Pectoral fin In fish, the fin just to the rear of the gill opening.

Pedal disc In sea anemones, the adhesive base of the columnar body. At the other end is the *oral disc*.

Pedicel A slender stalk that connects two objects.

Pedicellaria (plural: pedicellariae) In sea urchins and sea stars, a small pincer-like structure on the body surface.

Pelagic Living in the open sea.

Pelvic fin Usually found in pairs on the lower part of a fish's body, near the belly. Also called *ventral* fins.

Periostracum In mollusks, the generally fibrous organic material on the outside of the shell.

Periproct In urchins, the opening in the top of the test through which waste matter passes; the anus.

Peristome On the underside of urchins and sand dollars, the opening in the center of test that serves as the mouth.

Pheromone A substance that is produced by one animal in order to chemo-communicate with another. Example: A female crab releases a pheromone to attract a male.

Phylum (plural: phyla) In taxonomy, a major division of plants or animals. A phylum is divided into classes, then into species.

Phytoplankton The plant organisms in plankton, which may also consist of minute animals.

Pincers Claws; appendages for grasping.

Pinnate Branched in a feather-like pattern.

Plankton Small organisms that drift with the current and are suspended in the upper part of any body of water. May be plant or animal.

Pleopod In crustaceans, an abdominal appendage that is used for swimming, holding egg clusters, and breathing.

Podium (plural: podia) In echinoderms, a "tube foot" that is used for locomotion and feeding.

Polychaete A class of worms that are externally segmented and have bristles on the surface of their bodies.

Polyp A sedentary form of cnidarian. It has a cylindrical trunk that's fixed at one end; at the other end is the mouth, which is surrounded by tentacles. Example: sea anemone or hydroid.

Posterior At or near the rear end of the body.

Preopercle In fish, the most anterior of the opercular series of bones; the bone of the cheek.

Proboscis A snout or trunk whose structure varies in different phyla.

Pycnogonid A class of marine arthropods called sea spiders.

R

Radial Symmetry A type of geometric organization in which identical parts or rays are arranged around a central point or shaft. Found in sea stars, sea urchins, and jellyfish, among others.

Radioles The tentacles of some sedentary worms.

Radula A ribbon-like band with transverse rows of teeth; often protruded through the mouth and used for scraping.

Rhinophores In nudibranchs, a pair of tentacles, often elaborate, on the upper surface of the head.

Ribs In mollusks, the radial lines running from the umbones to the lower or end margins of the valves or shells.

Rostrum In crustaceans, a forward prolongation of the carapace.

S

Sedentary Remaining in one area. Example: annelid worms, which don't leave their burrows.

Sessile Fixed tightly to the substrate, usually not capable of moving.

Setae (singular: seta) Bristles, especially those in annelid worms.

Sieve plate In echinoderms, the perforated plate on the body surface through which water enters or leaves the vascular system.

Siliceous Composed of or containing silica.

Siphon A tube. Bivalves generally have an *incurrent* and an *excurrent* siphon, which carry water into and out of the body. In tunicates, these are called atrial and branchial siphons.

Siphonoglyph In anthozoans (cnidarians), a groove down the side of the pharynx through which food passes to the digestive cavity.

Species An animal or plant population with similar characteristics and the capability of breeding with one another.

Spicules Small siliceous or calcareous structures that stiffen the body (or certain parts of the body) of some animals. Example: sponges.

Spine In fish, a stiff, sharp-pointed rib that supports the fin.

Spire In a snail, the area from the body whorl to the apex.

Statocyst In invertebrates, a sense organ that controls balance.

Stipe In algae, the stem or stalk.

Substrate The ground or other solid surface on which animals walk or to which they attach themselves.

Subtidal The area on the coast that is below the low-tide line.

Suture In a snail, the space (or line) where one whorl touches another.

Swim bladder The gas-filled sac whose main function is to maintain a fish's vertical position in the water.

Swimmeret In crustaceans, one of the small appendages of the abdomen.

Symbiosis A constant association between two species of organisms (includes commensalism, mutualism, and parasitism).

T

Taxonomy The scientific classification of living things.

Telson The terminal segment (tail) of a crustacean's abdomen.

Tentacles In cnidarians, the extension of a polyp or medusa that contains muscle cells and nematocysts, allowing the animal to capture prey.

Tergum In arthropods, the dorsal surface of a body segment.

Test Almost any hard outer covering of an organism or part of an organism. Example: sea urchins, sand dollars.

Thallus The solid structures (blades) of nonvascular plants.

Thoracic Pertaining to the area of the thorax.

Thorax In crustaceans and other arthropods, the middle portion of the body, between the head and the abdomen.

Trochophore A ciliated, planktonic larval stage of many invertebrate groups such as mollusks and annelids.

Tube feet In echinoderms, small appendages that are extensions of the water-vascular system. They sometimes have cup-like tips, which are used for locomotion and feeding.

Tubercle A small bump or low, rounded projection, larger than a papilla. Those on the surface of sea stars are typical.

Tunic The outer covering, often rather thick, of a solitary or social ascidian. To a large extent, it is composed of material chemically related to cellulose.

U

Umbo (plural: umbones) In bivalves, the beak above the hinge.

Umbilicus In snails, a small hollow at the base of the shell.

Umbrella The main mass of the medusae.

V

Valve In mollusks, one of the parts of the shell. Gastropods have one valve; bivalves, two; chitons, eight.

Veliger The planktonic larva of some mollusks.

Velum In hydromedusae, a veil-like membrane on the underside of the umbrella.

Vent Anus.

Ventral fin In fish, one of a pair of fins located on the belly, ahead of the anus. Position varies considerably from one species to another.

Ventral Referring to the underside of the body.

Vestigial Pertaining to an organ or body part that is only a trace or impression in the present organism, but was once an integral, functioning part of that animal's ancestral forms.

Viviparous Pertaining to females in which young are maintained internally before birth; live-bearing.

W

Wampum Pieces of shell that were used by Native Americans as money.

Water-Vascular System In echinoderms, the "hydraulic" system used for holding on, locomotion, and eating.

Whorl A circular arrangement of parts. In gastropods, one turn of the shell.

Wing In bivalves, a triangular projection or extension on the plane of the hinge.

Z

Zoochlorellae Microscopic algae that live symbiotically in sponges and give them a green color.

Zooid In colonial animals, one of the individuals of the colony.

Zooplankton The animal organisms in plankton,which may also include plants.

Zygote A fertilized egg.

INDEX

Common names are those frequently used by the public. They are helpful but don't always mean the same thing from area to area. Some organisms have several common or even local names, which can lead to confusion. The scientific designation is often the more useful name. It consists of two parts. The first word is the genus and is always capitalized. The genus name is given to a group of organisms with similar physical characteristics. The second word is the species and is never capitalized. Within its genus, a species includes animals that are able to mate, reproduce, and create fertile offspring. Scientific names come from Latin and Greek roots; they are standard throughout the world, but many have been changed over time. An index of both common and scientific names is included here to assist the reader in identifying creatures found in this book.

COMMON NAMES

A

Acadian Hermit Crab, 162
Algae
  Crustose, 28
  Coral Weed, 24
  Dulse, 28
  Eel Grass, 28
  Green Fleece, 14
  Green Hair Weed, 16
  Hollow Green, 14
  Hooked Weed, 26
  Irish Moss, 26
  Knotted Wrack, 20
  Rockweed, 18
  Rough Tangle Weed, 24
  Sea Colander, 22
  Sea Lettuce, 16
  Southern Kelp, 22
  Spiny Sour Weed, 24
  Spiral Rockweed, 18
  Tubed Weed, 20
Alligatorfish, 246
American Eel, 226
Amphipod(s)
  Hedgehog, 152
  Skeleton Shrimp, 154
Ancula, Atlantic 96
Anemone(s)
  Frilled, 64
  Knobby, 68
  Lined, 56
  Ghost, 66
  Northern Red, 60
  Red stomphia, 62
  Rugose, 68
  Silver-Spotted, 58
Anemone Sea Spider, 146
Annelida, 132
Appendicularian, 216
Arthropoda, 144
Ascidian(s)
  Blood Drop Tunicate, 214
  Club Tunicate, 216
  Golden Star Tunicate, 210
  Northern White Crust, 210
  Orange Sheath Tunicate, 216
  Pink Sea Pork, 212
  Sea Peach, 214
  Stalked Tunicate, 212
  Sea Vase, 214

B

Badge Star, 202
Barnacle(s)
  Ivory, 150
  Northern Rock, 150
  Rough, 150
Basket Star, Northern, 204
Bass, Striped 230
Bay Scallop, 120
Beroe's Comb Jelly, 74
Bivalves
  Bay Scallop, 120
  Black Quahog, 122
  Blue Mussel, 116
  Common Jingle Shell, 122
  Common Oyster, 120
  Common Razor Clam, 126
  Deep-sea Scallop, 118
  Great Piddock, 128
  Horse Mussel, 116
  Iceland Scallop, 118
  Little Black Mussel, 118
  Quahog (Hard-shell Clam), 122
  Ribbed Mussel, 116
  Soft-shell Clam, 126
  Surf Clam, 124
  Truncate Soft-shell Clam, 128
Black Sea Bass, 232
Black Quahog, 122
Blood Drop Tunicate, 214
Blood Sea Star, 192
Blue Crab, 172
Blue Mussel, 116

Blue Shark, 220
Brachiopoda, 71
Brittle Star, Daisy 206
Boring Sponge, 34
Brown-Banded Wentletrap, 84
Brown Psolus, 181
Bryozoan(s), 71
  Red Crust, 76
  Sea Lace, 74
  Spiral Tufted, 76
Burrowing Anemone, 68
Bushy-Backed Nudibranch, 106

C

Cadlina, White Atlantic 100
Ceriantlhid, Northern, 68
Chalice Sponge, 36
Channeled Whelk, 96
Chevron Amphiporus, 74
Chiton(s)
  Dressed, 80
  Mottled Red, 80
Chordata, 208
Clam (see Bivalves)
Clam Worm,136
Clapper Hydromedusa, 42
Club Tunicate, 216
Cnidaria, 38
Cod, Atlantic 228
Coelentrata, 38
Colander, Sea 22
Comb Jellies
  Beroe's Comb, 74
  Common Northern Comb, 72
  Leidy's Comb, 72
  Sea Gooseberry, 72
Common Jingle Shell, 122
Common Northern Comb Jelly, 72
Common Oyster, 120
Common Palmate Sponge, 36
Common Periwinkle, 82
Common Razor Clam, 126
Common Sand Dollar, 186
Common Slipper Shell, 86
Common Spider Crab, 166
Coral
  Northern Stony, 58
  Red Soft, 56
Coral Weed, 24
Crab(s)
  Acadian Hermit, 162
  Blue, 172
  Common Spider, 166
  Flat-clawed Hermit, 162
  Green, 170
  Hairy Hermit, 160
  Jonah, 170
  Lady, 172
  Rock, 168
  Sand Fiddler, 174
  Toad, 166
Crumb Of Bread Sponge, 32
Crust
  Northern Whire, 210
  Red, 76
Crustose Algae, 28
Ctenophora, 70
Cunner, 232

D

Daisy Brittle Star, 206
Dead Man's Fingers, 54
Deep Sea Scallop, 118
Dogfish, Spiny 220
Dogwinkle, Atlantic 90
Dorid, White 102
Dressed Chiton, 80
Drill, Oyster, 90
Dulse, 28
Dwarf Ballon Eolis, 108

E

Eastern Mud Whelk, 92
Echinodermata, 176
Eel, American 226
Eel Grass, 28
Eight-Ribbed Hydromedusa, 48
Elegant Hydromedusa, 48
Eolis
  Dwarf Balloon, 108
  Robust Frond, 104
Eyed-Fringed Worm, 138

F

Fan Worm, 140
Fifteen-Scaled Worm, 136
Finger Sponge, 32
Fish(es)
  American Eel, 226
  Arctic Shanny,
  Atlantic Cod, 228
  Atlantic Herring, 226
  Atlantic Menhaden, 226
  Atlantic Spiny Lumpsucker, 250
  Atlantic Torpedo, 222
  Atlantic Wolffish, 238
  Black Bass, 232
  Blue Shark, 220
  Cunner, 232
  Fourspot Flounder, 252
  Goosefish, 228
  Ocean Pout, 238
  Longhorn Sculpin, 246
  Lumpfish, 248
  Northern Pipefish, 230
  Northern Puffer, 250
  Northern Sea Robin, 240
  Pollock, 228
  Radiated Shanny, 234
  Rock Gunnel, 236
  Rose Fish (Acadian Redfish), 240
  Sea Raven, 242
  Shorthorn Sculpin, 244
  Summer Flounder, 252
  Spiny Dogfish, 220
  Squirrel Hake, 230
  Tautog, 232
  Windowpane Flounder, 252
  Winter Flounder, 254
  Winter Skate, 224

Flat Slipper Shell, 86
Flat-clawed Hermit Crab, 162
Fleece, Green 14
Flounder(s)
  Fourspot, 252
  Summer, 252
  Windowpane, 252
  Winter, 254
Forbes' Sea Star, 192
Fourspot Flounder, 252
Frilled Anemone, 64

G

Golden Star Tunicate, 210
Goosefish, 228
Ghost Anemone, 66
Great Piddock, 128
Green Crab, 170
Green Fleece, 14
Green Hair Weed, 16
Green Sea Urchin, 184
Green Slender Sea Star, 198
Greenland Shrimp, 160
Greenland Wentletrap, 84
Grubby, 246
Gunnel, Rock 236

H

Hair Weed, Green 16
Hairy Doris, 102
Hairy Sea Cucumber, 182
Hake, Squirrel 230
Hedgehog Amphipod, 152
Herring, Atlantic 226
Hermit Crab(s)
  Acadian, 162
  Flat-clawed, 162
  Hairy, 160
Hollow Green Algae, 14
Hooked Weed, 26
Horned Krill Shrimp, 156
Horse Star, 202
Horseshoe Crab, Atlantic, 148
Hydroid(s)
  Snail Fur, 42
  Solitary, 40
  Tubularian, 40
  Wine-glass, 42
  Zig-Zag Wine-Glass, 42
Hydromedusae
  Clapper, 42
  Eight-ribbed, 48
  Elegant, 48
  Many-armed, 44
  Many-ribbed, 44
  White Cross, 46

I

Iceland Scallop, 118
Irish Moss, 26
Isopod
  Baltic, 152
  Hedgehog, 152
Ivory Barnacle, 150

J

Jellyfish(es)
  Lion's Mane, 52
  Moon, 52
  Stalked, 54
Johnston's Ornate Worm, 138
Jonah Crab, 170

K

Kelp, Southern 22
Knobbed Whelk, 96
Knobby Anemone, 68
Knotted Wrack, 20
Krill, Horned, 156

L

Lacy Tube Worm, 142
Lady Crab, 172
Lamp Shell, Northern, 76
Leafy Paddle Worm, 134
Leidy's Comb Jelly, 72
Lentel Sea Spider, 146
Leptomedusa, 44
Limpet, Tortoiseshell, 80
Lined Anemone, 56
Lion's Mane Jelly, 52
Little Black Mussel, 118
Lobed Moon Snail, 90
Lobster, Northern, 164
Long-Finned Squid, 130
Longhorn Sculpin, 246
Lumpfish, 248

M

Maned Nudibranch, 114
Many-armed Hydromedusa, 44
Many-ribbed Hydromedusa, 44
Menhaden, Atlantic 226
Molluska, 78
Montague's Shrimp, 158
Moon Jelly, 52
Moon Snail, Northern 88
Moss, Irish, 26
Mottled Red Chiton, 80
Mussel(s)
  Blue, 116
  Little Black, 118
  Northern Horse, 116
  Ribbed, 116
Mysid Shrimp, 156

N

Naked Sea Butterfly, 98
Nemertean Worms, 70
New England Dog Whelk, 92
Northern Basket Star, 204
Northern Cerianthid, 68
Northern Horse Mussel, 116
Northern Lamp Shell, 76
Northern Lobster, 164
Northern Moon Snail, 88
Northern Pipefish, 230
Northern Puffer, 250
Northern Red Anemone, 60
Northern Rock Barnacle, 150
Northern Searobin, 240
Northern Sea Star, 196

Northern Stony Coral, 58
Northern White Crust, 210
Nudibranch(s)
- Atlantic Ancula, 106
- Bushy-backed, 106
- Dwarf Balloon Eolis, 108
- Hairy Doris, 102
- Maned, 114
- Red-gilled, 108
- Rim-backed, 104
- Robust Frond Eolis, 104
- Rough-mantled, 100
- Salmon-gilled, 112
- White Atlantic Cadlina, 100
- White Dorid, 102

O

Ocean Pout, 238
Orange Sheath Tunicate, 216
Orange-footed Cucumber, 180
Oyster Drill, 90

P

Periwinkle(s)
- Common, 82
- Rough, 82
- Smooth, 82

Piddock, Great 128
Pink Sea Pork, 212
Pipefish, Northern 230
Plankton Worm, 134
Polar Sea Star, 198
Polar Shrimp, 158
Pollock, 228
Pout, Ocean 238
Psolus, Scarlet 178
Puffer, Northern 250
Purple Sea Urchin, 182
Purple Sponge, 34

Q

Quahog (Hard-shelled Clam), 122
Quahog, Black 122

R

Radiated Shanny, 234
Razor Clam, Common 126
Red Beard Sponge, 34
Red Crust, 76
Red Soft Coral, 56
Red Stomphia, 62
Red Terebellid Worm, 138
Red-gilled Nudibranch, 108
Rhynchocoela, 70
Ribbed Mussel, 116
Rim-backed Nudibranch, 104
Robust Frond Eolis, 104
Rock Crab, 168
Rock Gunnel, 236
Rockweed, 18
- Spiral, 18

Rose Fish, 240
Rough Barnacle, 150
Rough-mantled Nudibranch, 100
Rough Periwinkle, 82
Rough Tangle Weed, 24
Rugose Anemone, 68

S

Sabellid (Fan) Worm, 140
Salmon-gilled Nudibranch, 112
Sand Collar, 88
Sand Dollar, Common, 186
Sand Fiddler Crab, 174
Sand Shrimp, 156
Scarlet Psolus, 178
Scallop(s)
- Bay, 120
- Deep Sea, 118
- Iceland, 118

Sculpin
- Longhorn, 246
- Shorthorn, 244

Sea Bass, Black 232
Sea Butterfly, Naked 98
Sea Colander, 22
Sea Cucumber(s)
- Hairy, 182
- Orange-footed, 180
- Scarlet Psolus, 178
- Silky, 182

Sea Gooseberry, 72
Sea Grape, 210
Sea Lace, 74
Sea Lettuce, 16
Sea Peach, 214
Sea Pork, Pink 212
Sea Raven, 242
Sea Robin, Northern 240
Sea Spider(s)
- Anemone, 146
- Lentel, 146

Sea Squirt (See Ascidians)
Sea Star(s)
- Badge, 202
- Blood, 192
- Forbes' Asterias, 194
- Green Slender, 198
- Horse, 202
- Northern Basket, 204
- Northern (Boreal), 196
- Polar, 198
- Smooth (Purple), 188
- Spiny Sunstar, 190
- Winged, 200

Sea Vase, 214
Sculpin(s)
- Longhorn, 246
- Shorthorn, 244

Shanny
- Arctic, 234
- Radiated, 234

Shark, Blue 220
Shorthorn Sculpin, 244
Shrimp(s)
- Greenland, 160
- Horned Krill, 156
- Montague's, 158
- Mysid (Opossum), 156
- Polar, 158

Sand, 156
Skeleton, 154
Silky Sea Cucumber, 182
Silver-Spotted Anemone, 58
Sinistral Spiral Tube Worm, 142
Siphonophore, 50
Skate, Winter 224
Skeleton Shrimp, 154
Slipper Shell
Common, 86
Flat, 86
Slime (Fan) Worm, 140
Smooth Periwinkle, 82
Smooth (Purple) Sunstar, 188
Snail(s)
Brown-Banded Wentletrap, 84
Channeled Whelk, 96
Common Periwinkle, 82
Common Slipper Shell, 86
Dogwinkle, 90
Eastern Mud Whelk, 92
Flat Slipper Shell, 86
Knobbed Whelk, 96
Greenland Wentletrap, 84
Lobed Moon, 90
New England Dog Whelk, 92
Northern Moon, 88
Oyster Drill, 90
Rough Periwinkle, 82
Smooth Periwinkle, 82
Stimpson's Colus, 98
Ten-ridged Whelk, 94
Waved Whelk, 94
Snail Fur Hydroid, 42
Soft Coral(s)
Dead Man's Fingers, 54
Red Soft Coral, 56
Soft-Shell Clam, 126
Solitary Hydroid, 40
Southern Kelp, 22
Spider Crab, Common 166
Spiny Dogfish, 220
Spiny Lumpsucker, Atlantic 250
Spiny Sour Weed, 224
Spiny Sunstar, 190
Spiral Rockweed, 18
Spiral Tufted Bryozoan, 76
Sponge(s)
Boring, 34
Chalice, 36
Crumb of Bread, 32
Finger, 32
Palmate, 36
Purple, 34
Red beard, 34
Warty, 36
Squid, Long-finned, 130
Squirrel Hake, 230
Stalked Jellyfish, 54
Stalked Tunicate, 212
Starfish (See Sea Star)
Stimpson's Colus, 98
Stomphia, Red 62
Striped Bass, 230
Summer Flounder, 252
Surf Clam, 124

T

Tautog, 232
Ten-Ridged Whelk, 94
Toad Crab, 166
Torpedo, Atlantic 222
Tortoiseshell Limpet, 80
Truncate Soft-shell Clam, 128
Tubed Weeds, 20
Tubularian Hydroid, 40
Tunicate (See Ascidians)
Twelve-scaled Worm, 134

U

Urchin(s)
Green Sea, 184
Purple Sea, 182

W

Warty Sponge, 36
Wentletrap
Brown-banded, 84
Greenland, 84
Whelk(s)
Eastern Mud, 92
Knobbed, 96
New England Dog, 92
Ten-Ridged, 94
Waved, 94
White Atlantic Cadlina, 100
White Cross Hydromedusa, 46
White Dorid, 102
Windowpane Flounder, 252
Winged Sea Star, 200
Winter Flounder, 254
Winter Skate, 224
Wolffish, Atlantic 238
Worm(s) Errant
Clam, 136
Chevron amphiporus, 74
Fifteen-scaled, 136
Leafy Paddle, 134
Plankton, 134
Twelve-scaled, 134
Worm(s) Sedentary
Eyed-Fringed, 138
Fan (Sabellid), 140
Johnston's Ornate, 138
Lacy Tube, 142
Red Terebellid, 138
Slime(Fan), 140
Sinistral Spiral Tube, 140
Wrack, Knotted 20

Z

Zig-Zag Wine-Glass Hydroid, 42

SCIENTIFIC NAMES

A

Acanthodoris pilosa, 102
Acmaea testudinalis, 80
Aeolidia papillosa, 114
Aequipectin irradians, 120
Aequorea macrodactyla, 46
Aequorea aequorea, 44
Agalma elegans, 50
Agarum cribrosum, 22
Alcyonium siderium, 54
Amaroucium pellucidum, 212
Amicula vestita, 80
Amphiporus angulatus, 74
Amphitrite johnstoni, 138
Anarhichas lupus, 238
Ancula gibbosa, 106
Anguilla rostrata, 226
Anomia simplex, 122
Anopodactylus lentus, 146
Arabacia punctulata, 182
Arctica islandica, 122
Ascophyllum nodosum, 20
Aspidophoroides monopterygius, 246
Asterias forbesi, 194
Asterias vulgaris, 196
Astrangia danae, 58
Aurelia aurita, 52

B

Balanus balanus, 150
Balanus eburnus, 150
Beroe sp., 74
Bolinopsis infundibulum, 72
Boltenia ovifera, 212
Bonnemaisonia hamifera, 26
Botryllus schlosseri, 210
Botrylloides violaceus, 216
Brevoortia tyrannus, 226
Buccinum undatum, 94
Bugula turrita, 76
Bunodactis stella, 58
Busycon canaliculatum, 96

C

Cadlina laevis, 100
Callinectes sapidus, 172
Campanularia sp., 42
Cancer borealis, 170
Cancer irroratus, 168
Caprella sp., 154
Carcinus maenas, 170
Centropristis striata, 232
Cerianthus borealis, 68
Chaetomorpha linum, 16
Chiridota laevis, 182
Chlamys islandicus, 118
Chondrus crispus, 26
Ciona intestinalis, 214
Cirratulus cirratus, 138
Cliona celata, 34
Clione limacina, 98
Codium fragile, 14
Colus stimpsoni, 98
Corallina officinalis, 24
Crangon septemspinosa, 156
Crossaster papposus, 190
Crassostrea virginica, 120
Crepidula fornicata, 86
Crepidula plana, 86
Cryptosula pallasiana, 76
Cucumaria frondosa, 180
Culpea harengus, 226
Cyanea capillata, 52
Cyclopterus lumpus, 248

D

Dendrodoa carnea, 214
Dendronotus frondosus, 106
Dendronotus robustus, 104
Desmarestia aculeata, 24
Diadumene leucolena, 66
Didemnum albidum, 210

E

Echinarachnius parma, 186
Edwardsia sp., 68
Ensis directus, 126
Enteromorpha intestinalis, 14
Epitonium rupicola, 84
Epitonium greenlandicum, 84
Eubranchus pallidus, 269
Eumicrotremus spinosus, 250

F

Fagesia lineata, 56
Filograna implexa, 142
Flabellina salmonacea, 112
Flabellina pellucida, 108
Fucus spiralis, 18
Fucus vesiculosus, 18

G

Gadus morhua, 228
Gersemia rubiformis, 56
Geukensia demissa, 116
Gorgonocephalus arcticus, 204

H

Halichondria panicea, 32
Haliclona oculata, 32
Haliclona permollis, 34
Haliclystus auricula, 54
Halocynthia pyriformis, 214
Halopsis ocellata, 44
Harmothoe imbricata, 136
Hemitripterus americanus, 242
Henricia sanguinolenta, 192
Hippasteria phrygiana, 202
Homarus americanus, 164
Hormathia nodosa, 68
Hyas coarctatus, 166
Hybocodon pendula, 40
Hydractinia echinata, 42

I

Idotea baltica, 152
Ilyanassa obsoleta, 92
Isodictya palmata, 36

L

Laminaria agardhii, 22
Laodicae undulata, 44
Lebbeus polaris, 158
Lebbeus groenlandicus, 160
Lepidonotus squamatus, 134
Leptasterias littoralis, 198
Leptasterias polaris, 198
Libinia emarginata, 166
Limulus polyphemus, 148
Littorina littorea, 82
Littorina obtusata, 82
Littorina saxatilis, 82
Loligo pealei, 130
Lophius americanus, 228
Lunatia heros, 88

M

Macrozoarces americanus, 238
Meganyctiphanas norvegica, 156
Melicertum octocostatum, 48
Melonanchora elliptica, 36
Membranipora membranacea, 74
Mercenaria mercenaria, 122
Metridium senile, 64
Microciona prolifera, 34
Mnemiopsis leidyi, 72
Modiolus modiolus, 116
Molgula sp., 210
Morone saxatilis, 230
Musculus niger, 118
Mya arenaria, 126
Mya truncata, 128
Myoxocephalus aenaeus, 246
Myoxocephalus octodecimspinosus, 246
Myoxocephalus scorpius, 244
Mysis sp., 156
Mytilus edulis, 116
Myxicola infundibulum, 140

N

Nassarius trivittatus, 92
Neptunea lyrata decemcostata, 94
Nereis virens, 136
Nucella lapillus, 90

O

Obelia geniculata, 44
Oikopleura labradoriensis, 216
Onchidoris bilamellata, 100
Onchidoris muricata, 270
Ophiopholis aculeata, 206
Ovalipes ocellatus, 172

P

Pagurus acadianus, 162
Pagurus arcuatus, 160
Pagurus pollicaris, 162
Pandalus montagui, 158
Paralichthys dentatus, 252
Paralichthys oblongus, 252
Paramphitoe hystrix, 152
Phakellia ventilabrum, 36
Pholis gunnellus, 236
Phyllodoce, 134
Placopecten magellanicus, 118
Pleurobrachia pileus, 72
Pleuronectes americanus, 254
Polinices duplicatus, 90
Pollachius virens, 228
Polycera dubia, 104
Polycirrus eximius, 138
Polysiphonia lanosa, 20
Porania insignis, 202
Prionace glauca, 220
Prionotus carolinus, 240
Psolus fabricii, 178
Psolus phantapus, 181
Pteraster militaria, 200
Pycnogonum littorale, 146

R

Raja ocellatus, 224
Rhodymenia palmata, 28

S

Sabella sp., 40
Sarsia tubulosa, 42
Sclerodactyla briareus, 182
Scophthalmus aquosus, 252
Sebastes fasciatus, 240
Semibalanus balanoides, 150
Solaster endeca, 188
Sphoeroides maculatus, 250
Spirorbis borealis, 142
Spisula solidissima, 124
Squalus acanthias, 220
Staurophora mertensi, 46
Stichaeus punctatus, 234
Stilophora rhizodes, 24
Stomphia coccinea, 62
Stronglyocentrotus droebachiensis, 184
Styela clava, 216
Syngnathus fuscus, 230

T

Tautoga onitis, 232
Tautogolabrus adspersus, 232
Terebratulina septentrionalis, 76
Tima formosa, 48
Tomopteris helgolandica, 134
Tonicella marmorea, 80
Torpedo nobiliana, 222
Tubularia crocea, 40

U

Uca pugilator, 174
Ulva lactuca, 16
Ulvaria subbifurcata, 234
Urophycis chuss, 230
Urosalpinx cinerea, 90
Urticina felina, 60

Z

Zirfaea crispata, 128
Zostera marina, 28

BIBLIOGRAPHY

Abbott, R. T. (1974). *American Seashells* (2nd ed.). New York: Van Nostrand Reinhold Company.

Abbott, R. T.; S. Peter Dance (1982). *Compendium of Seashells* No. E.P. Dutton.

Alldredge, A. (1982). *Life in the Sea, 'Appendicularians'*. San Francisco, CA: W.H. Freeman and Co.

Amos, W. H.; Stephen H. Amos (1985). *The Audubon Society Nature Guide Atlantic and Gulf Coasts.* New York: Alfred A Knopf.

Arboretum, C. (1972). *Seaweeds of the Connecticut Shore* (No. 18). Connecticut Arboretum.

Arnold, A. F. (1968). *The Sea-Beach at Ebb-Tide*. New York: Dover Publications, Inc.

Barnes, R. D. (1980). *Invertebrate Zoology* (Fourth ed.). Philadelphia: Saunders College/Holt, Rinehart and Winston.

Bavendam, F. (1980). *Beneath Cold Waters-The Marine Life of New England.* Camden: Down East Books.

Berrick, S. (1986). *Crabs of Cape Cod.* Brewster: Cape Cod Museum of Natural History.

Berrill, N. J.; Jacquelyn Berrill (1957). *1001 Questions Answered About the Seashore.* New York: Dover Publications.

Bigelow, H. B.; William C. Schroeder (1953). *Fishes of the Gulf of Maine.* Washington: U.S. Fish and Wildlife Service.

Bleakney, J. Sherman (1996). *Sea Slugs of Atlantic Canada and the Gulf of Maine.* Halifax, Nova Scotia: Nimbus Publishing and The Nova Scotia Museum.

Borradaile, L. A.; F. A. Potts; L.E. S. Eastham; J. T. Saunders (1961). *Invertebrata.* Cambridge: University Press.

Buchsbaum, R. (1976). *Animals Without Backbones.* Chicago: The University of Chicago Press.

Calder, D. R. Ph.D.; Margaret Collison Pridgen (1977). *Guide to Common Jellyfishes of South Carolina* (Sea Grant Marine Advisory Bulletin #11). South Carolina Sea Grant.

Crowder, W. (1959). *Seashore Life Between the Tides.* New York: Dover Publications, Inc.

Dawson, E. Y. (1966). *Marine Botany: An Introduction.* New York: Holt, Rinehart and Winston, Inc.

Dayton, P. K. (1971). Competition, disturbance, and community organization: the provision and subsequent utilization of space in a rocky intertidal community. *Ecology Monograph, 41,* 351-389.

Dayton, P. K. (1975). Experimental evaluation of ecological dominance in a rocky shore intertidal algal community. *Ecology Monograph, 45,* 137-159.

de Laubenfels, M. W. (1953). *A Guide to the Sponges of Eastern North America.* Miami: University of Miami Press.

Flood, P. R. (1991). *Architecture of, and water circulation and flow rate in, the house of the planktonic tunicate Oikopleura labradoriensis.* Manuscript, University of Bergen, Norway.

Fontaine, P. H. (1992). *Sous Les Eaux Du St-Laurent.* Quebec, Canada: Les Editions du Plongeur, Inc.

Gosner, K. L. (1971). *Guide to Identification of Marine and Estuarine Invertebrates.* New York: John Wiley & Sons, Inc.

Gosner, K. L. (1979). *A Field Guide to the Atlantic Seashore.* Boston: Houghton Mifflin Company.

Harvey, W. H., M. D., M.R.I.A. (1858). *Contributions to a History of the Marine Algae of North America.* Washington: The Smithsonian Institution.

Hendrickson, R. (1978). *The Ocean Almanac.* New York: Doubleday.

Hillson, C. J. (1977). *Seaweeds A Color-Coded, Illustrated Guide to Common Marine Plants of the East Coast of the United States.* University Park: The Pennsylvania State University Press.

Kingsbury, J. M. (1969). *Seaweeds of Cape Cod and the Islands.* Chatham: The Chatham Press Inc.

Kramp, P. L. (1959). *The Hydromedusae of the Atlantic Ocean and Adjacent Waters* (Dana Report No. 46). Carlsberg Foundation.

Larson, R. J. (Ed.). (1976). *Marine Flora and Fauna of the Northeastern United States, Cnidaria, Scyphozoa.* Washington, D.C.: NOAA Technical Report.

Lee, T. F. (1986). *The Seaweed Handbook.* New York: Dover Publications, Inc.

Madin, L. P. Ph.D. (1991). *Distribution and Taxonomy of Zooplankton in the Alboran Sea and Adjacent Western Mediterranean* (No. WHO-91-26). Woods Hole Oceanographic Institution.

Marshall, N., Olga Marshall (1971). *Ocean Life in Color.* New York: The MacMillan Company.

Meinkoth, N. A. (1981). *The Audubon Society Field Guide to North American Seashore Creatures.* New York: Alfred A. Knopf.

Milne, L., Margery Milne (1972). *Invertebrates of North America.* New York: Doubleday & Company, Inc.

Miner, R. W. (1950). *Field Book of Seashore Life.* New York: G. P. Putnam's Sons.

Morris, P. A. (1975). *A Field Guide to Shells of the Atlantic and Gulf Coasts and the West Indies.* Boston: Houghton Mifflin Company.

Nelson, J. S. (1984). *Fishes of the World* (2nd ed.). New York: John Wiley & Sons.

Rehder, H. A. (1981). *The Audubon Society Field Guide to North American Seashells.* New York: Alfred A. Knopf.

Robins, C. R.; G. Carleton Ray; John Douglass and Rudolf Freund (1986). *A Field Guide to Atlantic Coast Fishes of North America.* Boston: Houghton Mifflin Company.

Robins, C. R.; Reeve M. Bailey; Carl E. Bond; James R. Brooker; Ernest A. Lachner; Robert N. Lea; W.B.Scott (1991). *A List of Common and Scientific Names of Fishes from the United States and Canada* (5th ed.). Bethesda, MD: American Fisheries Society Special Publication No. 20.

Russell, F. S., F.R.S. (1953, 1970). *The Medusae of the British Isles.* Cambridge, England: Universtiy Press.

Scott, W. B.; Mildred G.Scott (1988). *Atlantic Fishes of Canada.* Toronto: University of Toronto Press.

Smith, R. I. (Ed.). (1964). *Keys to Marine Invertebrates of the Woods Hole Region* (1st ed.). Woods Hole, MA: Marine Biological Laboratory.

Taylor, W. R. (1966). *Marine Algae of the Northeastern Coast of North America.* Ann Arbor: The University of Michigan Press.

Teal, J.; Mildred Teal (1971). *Life and Death of the Salt Marsh.* New York: Ballantine Books.

Wahle, L. (1990). *Plants and Animals of Long Island Sound.* Groton, CT: Connecticut Sea Grant College Program.

Wheeler, A. (1975). *Fishes of the World.* New York: The MacMillan Company.

Yonge, C. M. (1963). *The Sea Shore.* London: William Collins Sons & Co. Ltd.

Zinn, D. J. (1984). *Marine Mollusks of Cape Cod.* Brewster: Cape Cod Museum of Natural History.

Zottoli, R. (1978). *Introduction to Marine Environments* (2nd ed.). Saint Louis: The C.V. Mosby Company.